Making the Common Core Writing Standards Accessible Through Universal Design for Learning

This book is dedicated to my family, friends, and colleagues who have inspired and supported me throughout the process of writing my first solo book. Firstly, I want to thank my collaborator, Nancy Aguinaga, who brainstormed and conceptualized with me, and helped me get through "the deadly block" to a sense of clarity about UDL and its relationship to the CCSS. Stay swanky Nancy! Second, I am so very very fortunate to work with people who are not only wonderful colleagues but excellent friends. Rachel Friedman Narr, Wendy Murawski, Vanessa Goodwin, and Sue Sears, thank you for always believing that I could write this, even when I wasn't sure. Your support, your dedication to the field of Special Education, and your commitment to students inspires me and makes me happy to go to work every day. Finally, thank you to my family. My sisters, Ginny and Beth Spencer, gave me my first lessons in writing, (Literally! When we played school!) and are always there when I need them. To my niece, Tillie, who designed the beautiful icons for this book, thank you for sharing your talent with me. And last but not least, thank you to my husband Layne Dicker. You are my rock, my love, my one and only.

Making the Common Core Writing Standards Accessible Through Universal Design for Learning

Sally A. Spencer

With contributions by Nancy Aguinaga

CORWIN
A SAGE Company

FOR INFORMATION:

Corwin
A SAGE Company
2455 Teller Road
Thousand Oaks, California 91320
(800) 233-9936
www.corwin.com

SAGE Publications Ltd.
1 Oliver's Yard
55 City Road
London EC1Y 1SP
United Kingdom

SAGE Publications India Pvt. Ltd.
B 1/I 1 Mohan Cooperative Industrial Area
Mathura Road, New Delhi 110 044
India

SAGE Publications Asia-Pacific Pte. Ltd.
3 Church Street
#10-04 Samsung Hub
Singapore 049483

Printed in the United States of America

A catalog record of this book is available from the Library of Congress.

ISBN 978-1-4833-6947-1

Acquisitions Editor: Jessica Allan
Associate Editor: Kimberly Greenberg
Editorial Assistant: Cesar Reyes
Production Editor: Amy Schroller
Copy Editor: Jared Leighton
Typesetter: C&M Digitals (P) Ltd.
Proofreader: Dennis W. Webb
Indexer: Jean Casalegno
Cover Designer: Michelle Kenny
Marketing Manager: Amanda Boudria

This book is printed on acid-free paper.

15 16 17 18 19 10 9 8 7 6 5 4 3 2 1

Contents

About the Author

Sally A. Spencer, EdD, is an Associate Professor in the Department of Special Education at California State University, Northridge, where she teaches courses in assessment, special education teaching methods, reading instruction, and collaborative processes. Prior to that, she was a special education teacher for the Los Angeles Unified School District, where she experienced the joys and challenges of teaching in self-contained special education classes, as a resource specialist, and as a co-teacher in a fully inclusive elementary school. In 2001 she was awarded Outstanding Special Educator of the Year by the Southern California branch of the Council for Exceptional Children, and her heart is still in the classroom with the hundreds of students who touched her life and taught her everything she knows about special education. Sally is a presenter nationally on the subject of teaching reading to students with mild to moderate disabilities and is published in the areas of reading instruction, collaboration, and inclusion. She is the co-author, with Wendy Murawski, of the Corwin best-selling book, *Collaborate, Communicate, and Differentiate: How to Increase Student Learning in Today's Diverse Schools.* She lives in Northridge, California, with her husband, three dogs, two cats, and two birds.

Introduction

This is a book about the Common Core State Standards (CCSS) for writing. But perhaps more importantly, it's a book about how to make the Common Core writing standards work for all students, including those with special learning needs. Why do we need this book? Let's face it—we all recognize that the new standards are in many ways more challenging than the old ones, and lots of teachers and school districts are anxious about how to make these demanding academic standards accessible to kids who aren't on the high end of the curve. For many of us, the question of how to teach the new standards to struggling learners, students with disabilities, and second language learners is a critical one and, honestly, a bit overwhelming. We know that to do the standards justice it can't just be the "same old same old" type of teaching we've been doing for decades.

In addition, although many school districts haven't yet begun to figure out how to make the new standards accessible for students with special needs, classroom teachers can't afford to wait! From day one, your classrooms will be filled with kids with a wide range of learning strengths and challenges, and you need to be equipped to make the CCSS comprehensible and meaningful to all of them. This book is designed to help classroom teachers painlessly meet the needs of the wide range of abilities in their classrooms through the application of Universal Design for Learning (UDL).

Why UDL? I believe passionately that UDL is the best, easiest, and most practical way to make curriculum accessible to the wide range of learners that teachers face in contemporary classrooms. I also love the inclusive and proactive nature of UDL. It leads us away from the retroactive differentiation that makes some kids different from the norm. "This is what I want to teach, but how can I make it work for Yolanda or Alex? What do they need that's different from the rest of the class?" Instead, we adjust our thinking up front so that everything we plan and teach is more broadly available to all of our learners (Center for Applied Special Technology [CAST], 2014). As a classroom teacher for many years, I believe that if we make UDL part of our thinking from the beginning, our classrooms will become more effective for all our learners *with the least amount of effort.* Thumbs up for that.

I have unbounded enthusiasm for UDL and for its potential to unlock the CCSS for all learners; and frankly, I'm excited about where the CCSS can take our students with special needs and how they can grow from the opportunity to learn in this new and different way. It's my belief that students with disabilities have been mired way too long in basic skills, and the previous academic standards in many states encouraged teachers to continue that focus on remediation over higher-level thinking. With the CCSS, the expectations have changed for everyone, not just for typical learners. You can see it right there in the introduction to the Common Core—right off the bat they address the unique requirements of kids with special needs. Here is a quote from the introduction to the CCSS English Language Arts Standards section on Key Design Considerations: "The Standards should also be read as allowing for the widest possible range of students to participate fully from the outset and as permitting appropriate accommodations to ensure maximum participation of students with special education needs. For example, for students with disabilities *reading* should allow for the use of Braille, screen-reader technology, or other assistive devices, while *writing* should include the use of a scribe, computer, or speech-to-text technology. In a similar vein, *speaking* and *listening* should be interpreted broadly to include sign language" (National Governors Association Center for Best Practices, Council of Chief State School Officers, 2010).

This is a momentous change and a significant acknowledgment of kids whose needs lie outside those we consider typical. It is also a substantial step forward for the teaching field as a whole. Even today it's not uncommon to find teachers who believe that if a child can't take a pen in hand and write an essay on a piece of paper, then he or she is not really a writer. What the CCSS is telling us is that *this isn't true.* If a student can organize her thoughts in a meaningful way and dictate them into a machine or to another human being, *she is a writer* and should officially be recognized as such. This doesn't, of course, mean that students with special needs should not receive remediation where they need it, but it does mean that we need to begin thinking about academic standards in a different way. A student may need remediation in spelling skills, for example, but still be able to organize and compose thoughts on a high level when spelling is supported. The CCSS is asking us to use technology as a tool to help students work on the higher-level skills of composition, which can then free us to spend time on the remediation of basic reading, spelling, or other foundational skills our students may need. This is a progressive way of thinking and one that acknowledges the potential of technology to change the way we teach as well as the way students express their learning. It is also completely aligned with the principle of UDL, as you will see when you delve further into this book.

I believe the focus on writing is one of the most intriguing aspects of the CCSS. To that purpose, this book covers both the CCSS writing standards and the CCSS language standards, where critical foundational skills in writing such as grammar, syntax, and punctuation are found. All of these skills are important parts of writing proficiency for students, including students with special needs, and I am eager to offer teachers a myriad of hands-on strategies and activities that can help make these proficiencies meaningful and accessible to all the kids in their classrooms. It seems to me that the time is just right to shine a light on the teaching of writing to kids with special needs through the lens of the CCSS and UDL.

So I'm excited!! I'm excited about the potential, I'm excited about the direction, I'm excited about the new considerations for kids with special needs, and I'm excited that our classrooms are taking a new direction. I'm thrilled that the new standards really do look forward instead of backward—that they are asking us to change what "school" looks like and shaking us out of that old 1950s model. I think special educator Rick Lavoie says it best: "We've been doing closed-book teaching in an open-book world." It's time to take a critical look at what we're teaching, how it meets the needs of kids, and whether it prepares them for life in the twenty-first century (Lavoie, 2007). I believe the Common Core Standards are a positive step in that direction.

This book is designed to help you accomplish that step into the twenty-first century by making your writing instruction in the CCSS accessible for your students with special educational needs. That means all different kinds of special needs, including low-incidence disabilities like blindness and deafness, students with autism, and also students whose needs aren't a disability, for example second language learners, who do need special consideration in the classroom but who are in no sense disabled. I will also put a strong focus on children with learning disabilities, since they constitute the vast majority of children with disabilities in our schools today.

In addition, this book will provide you with strategies to use across the range of Grades K–12. Because the CCSS are so well designed, it's often possible to take a strategy from a primary grade and adapt it up to middle school and even into high school in many cases. That's a testament to the clever spiralling of the CCSS writing and language standards.

There is a lot of special content in this book to help make the CCSS and UDL come alive for you as you read. In each chapter, you will find Insider Tips, which give you a little bit more detail about how to "make it work" in your classroom. Every chapter also has Teacher Tales and Student Sketches, which bring you actual classroom examples of the principles discussed, featuring real teachers and real kids. There are lots of Web Treasures scattered throughout the book, providing you with links to find resources, applications, and information on line. And finally, you'll find lots of reproducible pages that you can copy and use in your classroom.

UDL is sometimes spoken about as a "special education thing," but in fact, UDL is designed to make content more accessible and engaging for everyone, including students all along the spectrum of ability. However, this book is for teachers, and the truth is that teachers are worried about how to make the Common Core work for students with special needs. UDL is designed to help relieve the stigma of labels, but in the real world, schools still use labels, and teachers still get students who are identified with disabilities. Since I want this book to be practical for teachers, I am committed to making it real. I'm not going to ignore the fact that we have students with disabilities in our classes; I will talk about their specific learning needs and provide strategies to address them. Sometimes I'll talk about students with disabilities, sometimes students with special needs, and sometimes struggling learners, but in essence, what I'm giving you are strategies that will help you reach all your students, no matter their learning profile.

So without further ado, let's jump in. I hope as you read you will be engaged, entertained, and most importantly, *prepared* to make all your students better, more proficient writers through the CCSS and UDL. I salute you, the classroom teacher, who is committed to making your instruction work for all your kids. You are the future of education in America, and it is to you that this book is respectfully and humbly dedicated.

The Big Deal About Writing

1

Writing.

For many teachers, there is a long drawn-out sigh that follows the mention of this topic. Writing . . . sigh . . . It is and historically always has been a tough subject to teach.

More than any other subject, writing is where I've seen students with disabilities struggle and fail in general education

©Jupiterimages/Thinkstock Photos

classrooms. I think of Gio, a great kid who struggled with the effects of ADHD and who had amazing thoughts rattling around in his head but couldn't get any of them on paper. I remember Caroline, whose ability to compose text was completely stymied by her inability to spell. However, when I think of writing, the student that sticks in my mind above all is Brian. Brian was the student who, one sunny afternoon in April, forever changed my perspective on what it means to be a struggling writer.

Brian was a sixth grader with a learning disability. When he was younger, he struggled mightily to learn to decode text, but by the time he got to sixth grade, his decoding had improved immensely. He could read and comprehend the sixth-grade books with only a little extra help, and although he was still working on developing grade-level word analysis skills and vocabulary, he was keeping up with the workload pretty well. Math was mostly a breeze for Brian; it had taken him a while to

TEACHER'S TALES

memorize his multiplication tables, but now that he had mastered them, he was quick to catch on to new concepts in math.

On this particular day, Brian had come to my resource room for help finishing up an essay for his class. After getting some guidance from me, he was quietly working on his own when all of a sudden, he slammed his pencil on the desk, yelled "Damn!" and buried his head in his arms. I was shocked—Brian was not a young man known for cursing or bad behavior, so obviously something was terribly wrong. I immediately ran over to him and was dismayed to see tears in his eyes as he picked up his head dejectedly.

"Miss Spencer, I can't believe it!" Brian cried. "I was working on my essay when all of a sudden, I forgot how to write the letter K. It's horrible!! I just forgot!! How can I be in sixth grade and forget something like that?" Sighing deeply, Brian put his head back on the desk, overwhelmed and discouraged.

I was as shocked as Brian. How could this happen? How could a sixth grader, who knows how to read, can spell well enough, and is a whiz at math, suddenly forget how to write a single letter? It's incomprehensible! Over the years, however, I began to truly understand the complexities of writing and to appreciate all the systems that have to work in tandem to make writing happen. Finally, Brian's experience started to make sense. To Brian, writing was a very, very big deal.

WHAT'S THE BIG DEAL FOR KIDS WITH DISABILITIES?

Writing is, indeed, a very big deal for many kids, especially for those with learning challenges and disabilities. In some ways, writing an essay is like constructing a building: you need exceedingly strong foundational materials, all of which need to be functioning exceedingly well in order for the building to stand. If a single beam or girder is faulty, the whole thing can tumble. Just like a building, writing involves a slew of foundational skills (spelling, vocabulary, fine motor skills, and sequencing, to name a few), all of which need to be functioning efficiently for a student's writing to succeed.

Additionally, for a student to be a competent writer, all of these foundational systems need to work simultaneously. That's the challenge of writing—it involves an enormous amount of cognitive and physical resources, all of which need to function *at one time*. If we return to our building metaphor, it's as though we are asking our kids to mix the mortar, lay the bricks, operate the steam shovel to dig the foundation, and bury the rebar, all at the same time. For those of us who write well, all of our foundational systems interact seamlessly to allow us to imagine, plan, sequence, recall, spell, and operate a pencil simultaneously as we get our thoughts on paper. For kids with disabilities, these coinciding demands are frequently overwhelming. This was the problem for Brian—it wasn't that this bright sixth grader didn't know how to write the letter K, but for him, the overall cognitive and physical demands of writing were so overwhelming that his whole system shut down. Even skills that he seemingly mastered long ago, such as writing individual letters, came crashing to a halt. His foundational materials crumbled.

THE PHYSICAL AND COGNITIVE DEMANDS EMBEDDED IN WRITING

Researchers have discussed and quantified the cognitive and physical demands of writing in different ways. Two of the most prolific and respected researchers in the area of writing for students with special needs are Karen Harris and Steve Graham from Vanderbilt University. Their work over the years has clearly delineated many of the elements that confound our struggling writers, and they provide a framework through which we can identify some of the elements that make writing such a BIG DEAL to many students. What follows are brief descriptions of some of the most impactful elements that can affect a student's ability to be a good writer, as well as student examples to help you visualize how each of these elements might present itself in a classroom. At the end of the chapter, you can find references to the work of Graham and Harris so that you may do some more in-depth reading if you choose.

Memory

Memory plays a significant and powerful role in a student's ability to write (Harris & Graham, 2013). I list it first because it is also an area of deficit for many students with learning disabilities and other special needs, so providing UDL options that support memory can make writing more accessible to a wide variety of learners.

Memory is not a simple or unified concept, and it can be broken down in many different ways (Medina, 2014); for example, cognitive scientists have identified episodic memory, motor memory, spatial memory, and declarative memory, among others. However, educators often organize memory into three principle categories: **short-term memory**, **working memory**, and **long-term memory**. Each of these types of memory has a discrete and profound impact on a student's ability to write.

Short-Term Memory. Short-term memory is the type of memory you use during the exact moment in time you are completing a task, for example, holding a phone number in your head while you dial the numbers. Short-term memory is generally believed to have the capacity to store about seven pieces of information at a time, although if information is "chunked," it can hold more. This is why phone numbers were designed with only seven numbers; later, when they added area codes, they chunked the numbers into three parts to aid with retention.

Immediately after you complete a task the material you were holding in short-term memory disappears, unless you take resolute steps to retain it. In classrooms, short-term memory is generally believed to affect tasks such as following directions, answering questions, or copying from the blackboard.

STUDENT SKETCH

I have had many students whose short-term memory was poor, but the one that jumps to mind is Carla, a student with a learning disability. Carla had a terrible time copying anything off the board or out of a book, so using resources such as word walls and dictionaries to help her write was both time-consuming and aggravating. Most of the time, she could only hold about two letters at a time in her short-term memory. Imagine Carla trying to copy the word extraordinary from the word wall—she would look up at the wall, see the first two letters, look down at her paper, and write them: E-X . . . Then she would look back up, scan to the place she left off, see the next two letters, look down, and write them: T-R . . . etc. It was an exercise in frustration. For Carla and many of my other students, this resulted in her using only short, easily recalled words in her writing, even though she had the expressive vocabulary to do more.

Working Memory. Working memory (sometimes called active working memory) is where we store and maneuver information as we are using it, often manipulating multiple components at once. In writing, the load on working memory is extremely heavy (Swanson & Berninger, 1996). For example, unless a student's spelling has become automatic (and thus has moved into long-term memory), she will have to use working memory to sound out and write down the sequence of letters in words, which can significantly impact writing fluency (Berninger, Nielson, Abbott, Wijsman, & Raskind, 2008). (Something to consider—if you are requiring students to write in cursive, there is an even higher demand on working memory, since the connections between letters in cursive writing vary according to the order of the letters in the words. That's just one of the reasons that cursive writing can be so difficult for kids with learning differences.)

Additionally, as she is writing, the student will have to recall and apply the rules of mechanics, including punctuation, capitalization, and paragraph formation, as well as the plot elements and the order in which they occur. At the same time, the student must also remember and apply grammatical and syntactical elements, such as tenses, pronoun usage, and/or contractions, as she writes. These are just some of the many elements that are required to work simultaneously when a student writes, and together they place an almost crippling demand on working memory for many students with memory deficits.

STUDENT SKETCH

One of the simplest demands on working memory yet often one of the most confounding for students with learning challenges is remembering the order of the words in a sentence. It sounds ridiculously straightforward, yet I remember Dafne, a young lady with autism, who would constantly complain that she couldn't remember what she wanted to write. She had strong fine motor skills and was able to form complex sentences in her head but couldn't hold them in her working memory long enough to get them on paper, and she usually ended up writing simpler sentences instead. As a result, her work rarely reflected her potential, and as you might imagine, writing an entire essay or story became extremely challenging.

Long-Term Memory. A student uses long-term memory to retrieve elements that have been memorized and stored for later acquisition. This process is tricky and depends on multiple factors, such as the quality of the encoding as well as the organization of the storage mechanisms—in other words, whether the student did a good job of memorizing the content he or she is now trying to retrieve. When writing, students must use long-term memory to recollect specific vocabulary words and their meanings, to remember how to spell challenging words, and to summon up language and grammar conventions (which they then apply using working memory). Long-term memory can also be taxed when trying to remember facts and details related to the subject about which one is writing.

STUDENT SKETCH

Toby, a tenth grader, is a good example of a young person whose writing was significantly impacted by long-term memory deficits. Toby had an exceptionally hard time recalling vocabulary. In fact, at age fifteen he was like me at age fifty-nine, forever getting "stuck" in his writing and his speech because he couldn't think of the word he needed to complete his sentence. Toby's long-term memory scores were significantly delayed; in tenth grade, his ability to recall a sentence after a time delay was at the first-grade level. Recalling vocabulary words, elements of a story, spelling of unusual words, or facts about a topic were all problematic for him, and as a result, his writing would often be stunted.

As you can see, memory, in all its forms, plays a huge role in the writing process. Since a significant percentage of students with learning disabilities have memory deficits, memory requirements alone can be overwhelming when a student is assigned a writing task. However, memory is not the only cognitive demand embedded in writing!

There are some wonderful resources out there to help you learn more about memory and its effect on learning. The Brain Rules website (http://brainrules.net/brain-rules-video) has a variety of videos and modules that are entertaining and very informative. You can also go to the All Kinds of Minds website to see their module on memory at http://www.allkindsofminds.org/memory-module. The more you can learn about the effects of memory and how to compensate for them, the easier it will be for you to understand the needs of many of your struggling writers.

Graphomotor Functions

As you no doubt have observed, many students have **graphomotor** (or fine-motor) skill delays that can overwhelm their cognitive resources as they write. For these students, the straightforward act of holding and manipulating a pencil takes up such a large proportion of their concentration when writing that they have difficulty accessing many other cognitive functions (Olinghouse, Graham, & Harris, 2010). As I think back on my years of teaching, I realize that the handwriting of many of my students had similar patterns. When they wrote by hand, the letters were malformed and awkward, and it often looked as though the letters were created by much younger students—evidence of a graphomotor deficit.

Raymond was a student whose writing was severely impacted by poor graphomotor skills. His printing in eighth grade looked like a second grader had written it, and he formed many of his letters from the bottom up. He never even tried to tackle cursive writing, as it was obvious to everyone that he didn't have the fine-motor coordination needed. Fine-motor deficits for students like Raymond (sometimes called dysgraphia) make the physical act of writing painfully slow and laborious, lowering the student's motivation to write. In addition, for Raymond, the mental

effort required to complete the physical act of writing overwhelmed his ability to simultaneously plan, remember, and compose written text.

Language

Sixty-six percent of students who are labeled learning disabled are three or more grade levels behind in reading (National Center for Learning Disabilities, 2011), and many students with other types of special needs, such as autism, intellectual disabilities, hearing loss, and ADHD, also struggle with reading. Accordingly, these students frequently read less than their peers—usually considerably less—and because they read less, they tend to also have delays in their knowledge of vocabulary and their understanding of language conventions. Renowned researcher Keith Stanovich (1986) tagged this phenomenon the Matthew Effect. As described in the book of Matthew in the Bible, the rich get richer and the poor get poorer, a concept uniquely applicable to struggling learners, particularly in terms of reading and language skills. Those who read well become stronger and more proficient, those who don't fall further and further behind. The global vocabulary and language deficits encountered by students with reading delays put them at a substantial disadvantage when they are trying to write.

STUDENT SKETCH

Some students with decoding problems will acquire vocabulary and language proficiency through listening; in these cases, language may not be such a confounding factor in writing. For others, listening comprehension is also an area of weakness, so their overall acquisition of these skills is seriously delayed. Sandra was a great example of just such a student. She had poor listening comprehension and poor decoding skills and, by ninth grade, was still reading at a fourth-grade level. As a result, her ability to express herself orally and in writing mimicked that of a much younger student, and she needed supports to help her improve the complexity and content of her writing. In Sandra's case, she was also an English learner, so her writing problems were even further compounded by lack of exposure to English vocabulary and grammar.

Ordering

Many students with special needs have problems with ordering—either ordering things in time (temporal ordering), sequence (sequential ordering), or ordering things in physical space (spatial ordering). Students need strong temporal and sequential ordering skills in order to put events in order in a story, put letters in order in a word, and to sequence words within sentences. For some students, spatial ordering can also be a troublesome element in writing.

Roschan could not for the life of him indent his paragraphs—he just couldn't organize his brain spatially in order to do it. Most of the time he didn't indent at all, but when he tried, he would end up indenting every sentence a little bit farther until he was writing on about an inch of paper. Despite strong higher-level thinking abilities, Roschan's spatial ordering deficits created a problem when he tried to manually write anything longer than a couple of sentences.

Higher-Order Cognition (Complex Thinking)

Higher-order thinking has been defined as the ability to evaluate, synthesize, and make meaning of complex new material. It helps us to apply our learning to new situations to solve problems and is the process that allows people to use creativity to present ideas in new ways. In writing, higher-order cognition helps students reinvent ideas in their own words and organize and categorize ideas into a logical whole using a recursive process that allows them to evaluate and revise their work (Harris & Graham, 2013).

Obviously, higher-order thinking is an important component of effective writing. For some students with disabilities, this piece is relatively effortless; for others, it is completely overwhelming. Some students have strong higher-order thinking capabilities, but their motor skills, language, and/or memory problems keep them from being able to get their ideas down on paper. For others, higher-order thinking—the ability to think deeply about their topic and organize those thoughts into a cohesive whole—is their biggest challenge.

Stephen, a student on the autistic spectrum, was a good example of a student with difficulties in higher-order thinking. He could spell very well and had mastery of a variety of language conventions, but because he struggled with complex thinking skills, his ideas tended to be simplistic and his writing development was inhibited. Stephen's writing had a lack of sophistication typical of a much younger student. If students can't access and use higher-order thinking as they are planning and completing writing tasks, they will struggle to coherently address age-appropriate topics in their writing.

THE BIG DEAL ABOUT WRITING

As you can see, there are many disparate elements that need to be synchronized in order for a student to write proficiently. No wonder this is an area of difficulty for so many kids, even those without disabilities! Jeffrey, one of my all-time favorite students, described it this way:

Writing is the very hardest thing for me. It seems like I can't keep all the pieces going at the same time. Sometimes I know what I want to say, but I can't remember how to spell the words. Sometimes I can't get the thoughts straight in my head. Sometimes I have it in my head, but it gets all mixed up between my brain and the paper.

The simultaneous cognitive and physical demands are competing for resources as Jeffrey writes, and on any given day, one may be overpowering the rest. So . . . what's the big deal about writing? For students with disabilities, it is unlikely that all of the different systems involved in writing will function together efficiently without some major supports. We will begin to look at examples of these supports in later chapters, but first, let's consider some of the specifics about the Common Core writing and language standards.

Research tells us that we can enhance retention of new ideas by reviewing them after learning, so at the end of each chapter, I will take the opportunity to glance back at some of the big ideas from the chapter.

WRAPPING UP THE BIG IDEAS

- Proficient writing requires efficient interactions between many different cognitive and physical systems. Many students with learning challenges struggle to make all the systems work together.
- Memory deficits make writing very difficult for some students, impacting their ability to recall vocabulary, compose text, and construct words and sentences as they write.
- Some students struggle with graphomotor functions, and this can diminish their ability to get their thoughts on paper.
- Students with reading delays often develop global language deficits that make it difficult to produce age-appropriate writing.
- Difficulties with ordering and higher-level thinking can both impact writing performance.
- Writing is a BIG DEAL for students with disabilities!

FOR FURTHER READING

Berninger, V. W., Nielson, K., Abbott, R., Wijsman, E., & Raskind, W. (2008). Writing problems in developmental dyslexia: Underrecognized and under-treated. *Journal of School Psychology, 46*(1), 1–21.

Graham, S., & Harris, K.R. (2011). Writing and students with disabilities. In L. Lloyd, J. Kauffmann, & D. Hallanan (Eds.), *Handbook of Special Education* (pp. 422–433). London, England: Routledge.

Harris, K. R., & Graham, S. (2013). "An adjective is a word hanging down from a noun": Learning to write and students with learning disabilities. *Annals of Dyslexia, 63*, 65–79.

Levine, M. (2003). *A mind at a time.* New York, NY: Simon and Schuster.

Levine, M. D. (1993). *Developmental variation and learning disorders.* Cambridge, MA: Educators Publishing Service.

Medina, J. (2014). *Brain rules: 12 principles for surviving and thriving at work, home, and school.* Seattle, WA: Pear Press.

Swanson, H. L., & Berninger, V. W. (1996). Individual differences in children's writing: A function of working memory or reading or both processes? *Reading and Writing: An Interdisciplinary Journal, 8*, 357–383.

Strolling Through 2
the Standards

"Ugh—I'm grading some papers for one of my 300 level classes and I get overwhelmed sometimes because I feel like there is so much they don't know in terms of writing and critical thinking. There is so much reteaching that needs to happen. . . . I feel horrible knowing that some of these students are graduating and they don't even know how to write a real research paper. :-("

What you see above is a message recently posted on Facebook by my friend Linda who teaches upper division students at a state university. It's clear from her impassioned words that, even at the university level, the controversy around writing proficiency (or lack of it) rages strong. She went on to ask if there was any literature I knew of that addresses how the education field is dealing with these issues. I was extremely pleased to be able to tell her about the new Common Core writing and language standards, and how they are designed to scaffold kids to writing proficiency beginning in kindergarten. Although it's going to be a while before she feels the effects at the college level, it made me so happy to be able to say that, yes, the K–12 community knows of the problem and is taking steps to correct it!

Thankfully, the creators of the CCSS weren't afraid to tackle the topic of writing competence head on, and as a result we now have a set of extensive and systematic K–12 standards designed to support students in becoming strong writers in preparation for higher education. I believe this is a huge step forward for teachers at all levels. It is also one of the primary differences between the CCSS and previous standards—whereas under No Child Left Behind writing was effectively downplayed as a critical component of literacy, CCSS recognizes writing as an equally important partner to literacy skills such as fluency, decoding, and comprehension.

WHAT DOES IT MEAN TO BE A GOOD WRITER?

One of my favorite college classes to teach is the introductory class to writing methods. I always begin by asking my students (who are getting teaching credentials in special education) to place themselves along a Value Line, marked by a piece of masking tape running the length of the hallway outside the classroom. At one end of the tape is a sign that says, *"I believe you can't be a good writer unless you have a solid mastery of mechanics such as grammar, spelling, and punctuation."* At the other end is a sign that says, *"I don't believe mechanics are important. Students can learn to be good writers without them."* I ask my teachers-in-training to place themselves along this continuum according to their beliefs, and then we discuss it.

The discussion is always passionate and lively—new teachers will argue their position as though it is the most important thing in the world, and in some ways, maybe it is! If teachers can't produce students who know how to adequately express themselves in writing, their students' futures will be seriously limited. Any teacher who cares about her students also cares about their writing ability.

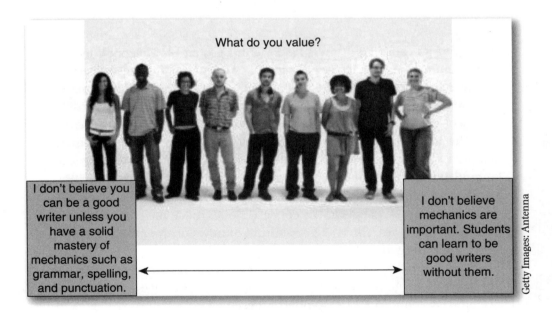

What do you value?

I don't believe you can be a good writer unless you have a solid mastery of mechanics such as grammar, spelling, and punctuation.

I don't believe mechanics are important. Students can learn to be good writers without them.

Getty Images: Antenna

But what does it mean to be a good writer? This is a philosophical issue on which teachers must take a stand, and it determines to a great extent how they will spend their time in the classroom. I believe there are two distinct elements to being a proficient writer: the mechanics, and the expression of ideas. Many K–12 students have a strength in one area and struggle in the other, and some have difficulty with both. What you value as a teacher, and what you choose to teach, will ultimately determine the types of skills your students will acquire.

At first it may seem like a simple discussion—obviously students need a balance of mechanics and ideas, right? Many teachers (and others) would argue that you can't get through life without the ability to organize your thoughts and express yourself clearly in writing. In addition, you need to be able to write with at least a passing mastery of spelling, punctuation, and grammar. Yet is that really true? Recently I hurt my shoulder, and typing causes me a fair amount of pain right now. As a result, I am using the dictation feature on my Mac to write this chapter, sitting with my feet elevated and my hands by my side, dictating my thoughts. Do I need to be able to think clearly, formulate my ideas, and use proper syntax and grammar? Absolutely! Do I need to be able to edit my work? Yes—as good as the dictation feature is, there are always some mistakes to be corrected, and I often change my mind about what I want to say. Do I need to have strong fine motor, capitalization, and spelling skills? Not really. I just wrote this entire paragraph without writing, typing, or spelling a word. In addition, as long as I say the word "period" at the end of my sentence, the computer capitalizes for me. TECHNOLOGY IS CHANGING EVERYTHING.

TEACHER'S TALES

Here's an example that may test your preconceptions about writing. I am lucky enough to count among my acquaintants author and advocate Jonathan Mooney. Jonathan is the author of two books, a nationally renowned public speaker, and a passionate advocate for students with learning disabilities. As an individual with a learning disability himself, he struggled in school and was told by multiple teachers that he would never amount to anything. At the end of fifth grade he was a nonreader and was completely disenfranchised from school. Luckily, Jonathan was able to turn things around through the efforts of his mother and a high school teacher who recognized his potential. He enrolled in Brown University and graduated with honors before beginning his career as an author and speaker.

To this day, the mechanics of writing are demanding for Jonathan. His spelling is poor, and capitalization and punctuation are challenging to him. When you receive an e-mail from Jonathan, sometimes it is hard to believe that a brilliant, eloquent adult wrote it. So does Jonathan need to improve his writing skills? Some people would proclaim loudly, "Yes", I, on the other hand, would advocate that Jonathan has learned to manage his writing, and when he needs to write in a professional manner he has tools to help him do so. However, when he's writing an e-mail to a friend, he lets it all hang out. If Jonathan were a student in one of my K–12 classes I would think carefully about how much time to spend on teaching him to master mechanics, and how much to spend on helping him develop and fine-tune his innate ability to express important ideas in a way that captivates his readers.

What does that mean for you as a teacher? It means that your philosophical choices about writing instruction are critically important, particularly for students who may have challenges and/or disabilities in writing. Writing is an intricate and multilayered task, and teaching students how to write is even more complex. As a teacher, you will have to make thoughtful and informed choices about how to focus your writing instruction, where to spend your time, and what you ultimately value in a writer. To complicate the task even more, this choice may not be the same for all students. Luckily, the Common Core is here to help!

CCSS WRITING AND LANGUAGE

As if they could read my mind, the writers of the Common Core recognized the dichotomy between ideas and mechanics and built the standards to support teachers in making that differentiation. The Common Core Writing Standards (http://www.corestandards.org/ELA-Literacy/W/introduction) focus on the *ideas*. They guide students in mastering different genres of writing and support them in learning how to use research and textual evidence to create and edit high-quality written products. Conversely, the Common Core Language Standards (http://www.core standards.org/ELA-Literacy/L/introduction-for-k-5) are focused on the *mechanics*, as they are applied to both written and spoken language. Together, these two sets of standards create a blueprint to help teachers build strong writers in their classrooms, and they provide a carefully scaffolded series of skills and concepts designed to support students in becoming proficient writers.

The Writing Standards: Vertically and Horizontally Aligned

When you're examining academic standards to see how they will work for you as a teacher, the vertical alignment from grade to grade is very important; it is really helpful if the progression of skills is clear and systematic from one grade to another. The Common Core writing and language standards both have an explicit and well-designed progression of skills that is easy to follow through the grade levels. This not only helps teachers understand where the kids came from and where they are going, but is of immense aid in figuring out how to differentiate instruction and build in supports for struggling learners. For example, if in sixth grade you are teaching your kids to use words and phrases to clarify relationships between claims (W.6.1.c) and you have a student who doesn't have the foundational understanding to tackle that yet, it is advantageous that standard W.4.1.c (the fourth grade standard in that strand) focuses on using words and phrases to link opinions and reasons. Working on that foundational skill is a reasonable accommodation that can help your student progress efficiently toward grade level proficiency.

The Four Big Ideas of Common Core Writing

The Common Core Writing Standards are built around four big ideas: *Text Types and Purposes, Production and Distribution, Research to Build and Present Knowledge,* and *Range of Writing.* Think of the four big ideas as **what students need to know how to do** to be college and career ready by the end of high school. Table 2.1 outlines each of these ideas.

The Common Core Writing Standards are focused around three primary types of writing: arguments, informational text, and narratives.

Table 2.1 The Big Ideas in CCSS Writing

The Four Big Ideas of the Common Core Writing Standards	
Text Types and Purposes	The CCSS identifies that students need to know how to write three different types of text: Writing arguments (W.1), informational writing (W.2), and narrative writing (W.3). The writers of the standards recognized that argument and information are the two primary types of writing done in the workplace, so they shifted the focus away from narrative writing.
Production and Distribution	The second big idea covers clarity of writing (W.4); the process of planning, editing, and revising work (W.5); and using technology to publish written work (W.6).
Research to Build and Present Knowledge	Skills related to conducting research (W.7), gathering and evaluating information (W.8), and supporting analysis with evidence (W.9) are greatly valued in higher education and are the focus of the third big idea of Common Core writing.
Range of Writing	The fourth big idea asks students to apply the writing skills across a variety of purposes and audiences, such as writing letters, reports, blogs, etc.

This is another tremendous shift, as a large percentage of writing instruction, particularly at the elementary level, used to be focused on narrative writing. The CCSS recognizes that once we are out of school, the primary type of writing needed for college and career is not the writing of stories; in fact, only a very few of us will have the pleasure of becoming professional fiction writers. Instead, for adults it's critically important that we know how to gather information from various text sources, evaluate the quality of the information, and present it clearly and succinctly. For those of us who write as part of our work, this is the type of writing in which we generally engage. Table 2.2 summarizes each of these three types of writing.

Like the other language arts standards, the Common Core Writing Standards are aligned in a horizontal direction: each standard connects and interacts with the other writing standards at that grade level. This, too, can be helpful to teachers. Just as writing involves the simultaneous

Table 2.2　The Three Types of Writing in the CCSS

Standard W.1: Writing Arguments

- Standard W.1 puts emphasis on the use of evidence to support well-reasoned claims. It shifts the focus away from persuasive writing, which is characterized by emotional appeal and self-interest, to logic, reasonableness, and proof. This kind of writing is utilized heavily in university courses, as well as in professions such as journalism, law, higher education, and politics. By high school, students are expected to not only form a cogent and well-supported argument, but to be able to clearly express the opposite point of view as well.

Standard W.2: Informational Writing

- Informational writing is what students might use to write reports, research briefs, summaries, book reports—any writing that is a statement of factual information. Obviously, the application for this in the work world is broad. Workers might have to write reports about productivity, summarize the results of surveys or conferences, or write manuals for the operation of equipment; in fact, informational writing is probably the most common type of writing in employment settings.

Standard W.3: Narrative Writing

- Narrative writing is generally organized around the passage of time and conveys events, either real or fictional. Formerly, about 80% of the reading and writing done in elementary school was narrative, but the Common Core has shifted that balance dramatically. Not all types of creative writing are included in the CCSS; for example, many types of poetry are left to the discretion of the teacher to include in the curriculum.

application of a lot of different skills, teaching writing also involves multiple elements. So whether you are teaching secondary students to write arguments or elementary students to write opinions (W.1), you will also need to teach your students how to effectively use evidence to support their arguments and opinions (W.8), and how to use technology to publish their work (W.6). Each grade level adds a little more structure, and increases the expectations for application of the skills across the standards. In Figure 2.1 you can see the anchor writing standards organized underneath each big idea.

The writing standards include complex yet thoughtful associations among a variety of types of writing and writing skills, and it is exactly this complexity that makes writing such an area of challenge for many students with special needs. Significantly, these standards don't include writing conventions such as grammar and punctuation, which are found in the language standards, and which add another layer of complexity to the task of writing.

Figure 2.1 The Common Core Writing Standards

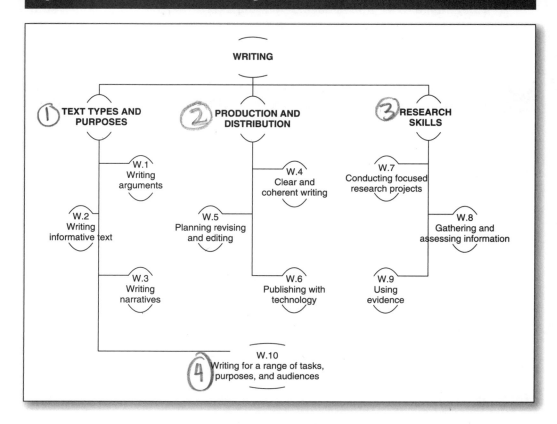

The Language Standards: A vertical progression of skills

Like the writing standards, the language standards are vertically aligned to provide a scaffolded series of skills that support student growth and differentiated instruction. Unlike the writing standards, the language standards only have three big ideas: *Conventions of Standard English, Knowledge of Language,* and *Vocabulary Acquisition and Use.* Once again, these big ideas represent **what the students need to know** about language to be college and career ready by the end of high school. See Figure 2.2 for a graphic depiction of these big ideas.

As can be seen in the figure, there are a total of six standards subsumed under these three big ideas. In the early grades, there is a heavy emphasis on the standards related to conventions. Students in Kindergarten through third grade will receive a lot of instruction on English grammar and usage (L.1), including skills such as verb tense, use of adjectives, conjunctions, and sentence types. They will also focus intensively on capitalization, spelling, and punctuation rules (L.2). The standard related to knowledge of language (L.3) doesn't begin until second grade and receives more intensive focus as students get older. As students move into middle and high school, the priorities shift toward vocabulary use (L.4), figurative language (L.5), and academic language (L.6). Table 2.3 presents a summary of each of the big ideas and the six Common Core anchor language standards within them.

Figure 2.2   The Big Ideas of the Common Core Language Standards

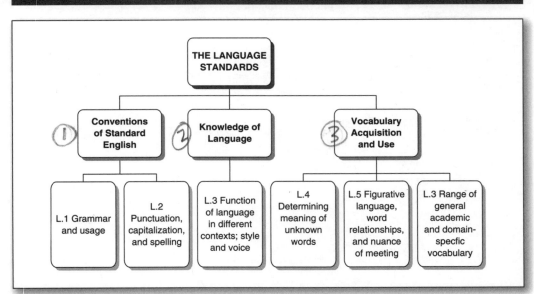

Table 2.3   A Summary of the Common Core Language Standards

Common Core Language Standards		
Conventions of Standard English	**L.1: Demonstrate command of conventional English grammar and usage.**	This standard helps students build competency in using basic parts of speech such as nouns, verbs, adjectives, and pronouns when they write and speak. In later grades it focuses on formal language use such as active and passive voice, verb forms, and clauses.
	L.2: Demonstrate command of capitalization, punctuation, and spelling.	This standard is heavily stressed in the early grades, but gradually diminishes over time, until by high school there are only one or two areas of focus. By sixth grade it is assumed that a student can capitalize and spell correctly, and a few advanced punctuation skills are taught throughout middle and high school.
Knowledge of Language	**L.3: Knowledge of language.**	Beginning in second grade, students are expected to develop an understanding of the difference between formal and informal language. As they get older, this standard asks them to master sentence patterns, tone, mood, style, and voice.
	L.4: Determine or clarify the meaning of unknown words.	Very early on, students are asked to use context to figure out the meaning of unknown words. This expectation continues throughout the grades. As students get older, knowledge of Greek and Latin roots, affixes, and the use of reference materials are all stressed as tools for vocabulary acquisition.
Vocabulary Acquisition and Use	**L.5: Understand figurative language, word relationships, and nuance in word meanings.**	This standard helps students better understand vocabulary by learning about synonyms and antonyms, idiomatic language, and the shades of meaning between similar words.
	L.6: Acquire and accurately use academic and domain specific words.	Although in the early grades this standard focuses on acquiring language through reading and conversation, after third grade there is an expectation that students will learn complex academic vocabulary that spans domains, as well as domain specific vocabulary in each of the subject areas.

SHIFTS IN THE COMMON CORE

Quite a bit has been written about the "six shifts" in instruction that are embedded in the Common Core. Although I am not going to go into them in depth here, I will briefly discuss how some of these shifts impact writing instruction, and thus your classroom. If you would like to dig deeper into the thinking behind the development of the Common Core, the New York State Department of Education has a website with videos and transcripts from a two-hour presentation by David Coleman (2011), one of the chief architects of the CCSS. You can access it here: http://usny.nysed.gov/rttt/resources/bringing-the-common-core-to-life.html.

According to Coleman, the two most commonly taught types of writing in high schools have been personal narratives and personal opinions. I love this quote from his speech: "It is a rare working environment in which someone says, 'Johnson, I need a market analysis by Friday, but before that I need a compelling account of your childhood.'"

The CCSS changes the focus of writing instruction significantly. As Coleman puts it, "Common Core requires students to read like detectives and write like reporters." What does it mean to teach kids to write like reporters? It means that they need to spend time digging deeply into expository text and pulling out information. Then they need to use that information to create logical and well structured argumentative and informational writings. They need to be able to take what they have read, synthesize it, put it in their own words, and use it to form thoughts of their own.

In addition, the Common Core puts an intensive focus on academic vocabulary. More specifically, the standards direct teachers to teach tier two academic words that are applied across content areas and subjects, such as *consequential* or *regulate*, as well as vocabulary specific to particular curricular domains.

Obviously, these shifts will require teachers to have some new strategies and tools in their classrooms. That's what this book is all about! Before we begin actually exploring those tools though, we need to learn a little bit about Universal Design for Learning, the framework that we will use to apply them. The next chapter will introduce you to UDL, and then we will jump into classroom strategies in earnest.

WRAPPING UP THE BIG IDEAS

- In order to be strong teachers of writing, teachers need to decide what they value in terms of writing proficiency. That decision will have a huge impact on how they spend their time in the classroom.

- The Common Core Writing Standards are focused on expression of ideas, including different writing genres and purposes. The Language Standards are focused on mechanics, including vocabulary acquisition.
- The writing standards have horizontal alignment, as well as vertical alignment across the grade levels, and are organized around three primary types of writing: argument, informational, and narrative.
- There are six language standards organized under three big ideas: conventions, knowledge of language, and vocabulary.
- Common Core requires students to "write like reporters": they need to be able to research, synthesize, and integrate ideas from a variety of text sources.

FOR FURTHER READING

Calkins, L., Ehrenworth, M., & Lehman, C. (2012). *Pathways to the Common Core: Accelerating achievement.* Portsmouth, NH: Heinemann.

Coleman, D. (2011, April). *Bringing the Common Core to life.* Paper presented at a meeting of the New York State Department of Education, Albany, NY.

read like detectives
write like reporters

Universal Design for Learning

3

Giulia Forsythe https://www.flickr.com/photos/gforsythe/9101797199/in/photolist-

WHAT THE HECK IS UDL?

Imagine this scenario: It is 1975, and you are catching a plane to go to Miami, where you are going to go on a two-week Caribbean cruise. You have two full-size suitcases packed with vacation wear, a shoulder bag with your personal hygiene and carry-on items, and a large beach bag. (After all, this is pre-9/11, so you can take as much stuff as you want!) You get to the airport and park on the second floor of the long-term lot only to find out there is no elevator or escalator. You are forced to make multiple trips up and down the stairs, dragging your cases over the steps and leaving them behind while you go to fetch the next one. You finally get everything to the bottom and hurry across the street to the terminal. In 1975 there are no curb cuts, so you have to drag your suitcases over the curbs and try to hold the terminal doors open (no electronic doors) as you struggle into the building. At this point, you are officially running late, and perspiration is running down your face in rivers. You make it to the counter, where there is a television playing an emergency announcement. The building is so noisy you can't hear the announcement, so you have no idea what is going on. You begin to panic.

Welcome to the world *before* universal design in architecture. Today, of course, it would be a different story. The parking garage would be equipped with an elevator for accessibility, and there would be curb cuts at every crosswalk so you could easily roll your suitcases across the street. You could push the electronic door button to enter without hassle, and if there was an emergency announcement on the television monitor, you could read the closed captioning to find out what was going on. Whew! Thanks to the universal design of modern airports, you can wrangle your luggage from your car to the check-in desk without breaking a sweat.

Universally designed buildings are designed and built to be accessible to individuals with disabilities right from the start; they don't need to be retrofitted because the accessibility features are intrinsic to the design. Although the features were designed for people with specific needs, many of us choose to use them to make our lives more convenient. *What was designed to make buildings accessible to people with disabilities turns out to be of service to us all.*

Universal Design for Learning (UDL) applies the same concept to the design of instruction. UDL was created at the Center for Applied Special Technology (CAST) in the mid-1980s and has evolved over time as a

tool to increase the effectiveness of inclusive classrooms. CAST brought together some of the sharpest minds in learning and technology to consider education in a new light. They realized that the thoughtful application of tools and technologies in a classroom can make learning much more accessible to students with disabilities; and lo and behold, just like curb cuts and automatic door openers, what was designed for children with disabilities turned out to be useful to every student in the classroom! The fundamental premise of UDL is providing flexible classroom options that are responsive to learner variability, and just like universal design in architecture, adaptability is intrinsic to the design; lessons are planned from the beginning with flexibility built-in, not retrofitted later. For a quick and engaging overview video about "UDL at a glance," check out http://www.udlcenter.org/resource_library/videos/udlcenter/udl.

Why Do We Need It?

Currently, most classrooms are designed to meet the needs of the kids in the middle of the learning and ability spectrum—we "teach to the middle." L. Todd Rose, an instructor in the Harvard College of Education and cofounder of Project Variability, describes the "myth of the average learner" as a misconception that is causing us to design classrooms that are only effective for a small percentage of our students. He likens it to a running coach who will only let his runners wear shoes that are designed for the average foot—size 8.5. In this scenario, only runners with feet close to size 8.5 would be able to reach their potential—everyone else would be constantly working at a disadvantage. Those with bigger feet would be in terrible pain and could only run for a short time, and those with smaller feet would be tripping and falling down all the time. No matter how strong their inherent abilities as runners, if the athletes' feet didn't fit the size 8.5 shoes, they would fail. The same is true with our classrooms. Dr. Rose suggests that the problem isn't the students, the problem is the way we design our teaching. If we are designing curriculum to fit the mythical "average" student, everyone else is left with a poor-fitting education (Repertoire Productions, 2013).

If you would like to hear Todd Rose speak about the "myth of the average learner" himself, I urge you to watch one of his YouTube videos. I recommend his presentation from the Ross Institute Summer Academy (https://www.youtube.com/watch?v=UVbFGjpfMUg) or his TEDx talk (https://www.youtube.com/watch?v=4eBmyttcfU4). Both are well worth the twenty minutes they take to watch, and they will give you a lot more insight into the concept of designing learning experiences for students beyond the range of "average."

If there is no such thing as average, then how does this affect our understanding of disabilities? Isn't "disability" a word for someone who falls outside the range we consider to be average? On the contrary, by definition, disability literally means the inability to do something. The athlete with a size 5 foot in a size 8.5 shoe would be "disabled" as a runner. A person like me with minimal artistic talent who is asked to paint a picture could be considered "disabled" as a painter. Likewise, a student with a learning pattern outside the range of what is provided for in his classroom is effectively "disabled" from learning. In fact, CAST believes that the design of the curricula can actually create a disability or remove one (CAST, 2014). A curriculum that is not universally designed does not take into account that students differ in abilities, interests, and learning processes and thus only meets the needs of the students whose abilities match the teaching. By limiting the way we present instruction and by teaching to the middle, we *create* students who are effectively disabled as learners.

One of the biggest "disablers" in our classrooms is print text. Our culture has long associated print text with knowledge, and for hundreds of years, our schools have been built around the delivery of print text—not surprisingly, since for most of our history it was all that was available. As we know, though, those times have changed. It is now possible to have an entire library in your back pocket, and in many cases, we not only carry the text with us electronically, but we can have it read aloud through the click of a button. No longer does the ability to access and decode print text define intelligence; the acquisition of information about the world has changed dramatically, and for students who lack a well-developed ability to interpret printed text, digital access is key. In a UDL classroom, teachers take advantage of the digital alternatives to provide options that open up the world of learning for all their students.

UDL is a pedagogical framework built on three foundational principles. Principle number one, ***engagement***, asks us to motivate and involve our students in learning by providing multiple and flexible options for their participation. Principle number two, ***representation***, invites us to present the content through an assortment of options that make it comprehensible to students with a range of personal traits, dispositions, and learning strengths. Principle number three, ***action/expression***, requires teachers to provide a variety of ways for their students to show what they know.

Nancy Aguinaga, an Associate Professor of Special Education at Southeast Missouri State University, worked with me to conceptualize the three elements of UDL and the interactions between them in a Venn diagram that we call "The UDL VennBrella." In our vision of UDL, *representation* and *expression* overlap where students practice with feedback; at this point, the process of teaching and the process of practicing what was learned become fluid and interactive. Additionally, we conceptualize *engagement* as a culture that overlies the elements like an umbrella, interacting with the other two elements in a reciprocal relationship. You'll read more about this in the next chapter.

Although all learning tasks require the interaction of many different parts of the brain, each of these principles is closely aligned to a particular network in our brain affiliated with learning: the affective network is related to engagement, the recognition network supports the principle of representation, and the strategic network is associated with the expression of knowledge (CAST, 2014). Let's take a closer look at these three principles one by one.

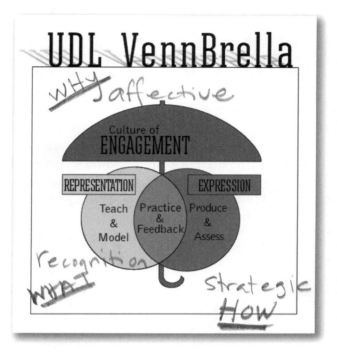

UDL Principle #1: Multiple Means of Engagement

As mentioned above, the UDL principle of engagement involves motivating students to learn. Under the principle of engagement, teachers are asked to consider what factors involve the students in learning and help them persist, even when learning gets tough. The principle of engagement asks us to give students the power to make choices about their learning, to select topics that are intrinsically meaningful to them, and to provide structures that help them regulate and organize their learning (CAST, 2014).

All of these factors are managed by the affective network of the brain—the area of the brain that controls how students feel about their learning. A student's affective response to an assignment influences whether he identifies it as important and whether he chooses to allocate physical and emotional energy to that assignment.

Most of us have experienced the excitement of a new job; at first, we are very excited about the potential of that job and get up every morning with a positive attitude and lots of mental energy. Our affective systems are firing productively! Over time, however, if the job doesn't live up to our expectations, our mental and physical energy will decline as we start each day. Our affect, or how we feel about the job, will soon have a negative influence on our ability to function in that job.

Let's think about engagement from a student's perspective. Raul, a tenth grader, has just begun an elective in journalism, and he is very excited about the idea of publishing his opinions in the school newspaper. Unfortunately, a week or so into the class, a couple of things happen to dampen that excitement. First, he finds out that he doesn't get to choose what he will write about—a student editor will be assigning him topics without his input. In addition, the teacher of the course has criticized his first two papers rather harshly, and he hasn't been provided with much support to make them better. Now, he is not only discouraged, but he is worried that when he publishes his work students might make fun of it. What started out as a positive, stimulating experience has quickly turned sour, and Raul's engagement in that class has rapidly declined. His affective processes are reacting to the threat of failure and embarrassment, and his motivation to persist is minimal.

The affective systems don't just react to threat or discomfort; they can also be impacted by other experiences. For example, if Raul fell in love two weeks into the semester, it could put a positive "shine" on everything around him, and he might be more motivated to work hard and impress his new heartthrob. On the other hand, if his parents split up, he could develop a pattern of disengagement and pessimism across all his classes. The affective network is influenced by a wide variety of life circumstances and has a powerful influence on everything that a student does in school.

CAST calls the engagement principle the *why* of learning. From a student's perspective, that might be translated as, "*Why* should I learn this? *Why* should I care about it? *Why* is this important in my life?" Engagement is about recruiting interest, motivating learners, and enhancing relevance, and CAST recommends giving students multiple ways to engage in their learning. Perhaps you might offer them choices about when and how to complete an assignment—they could choose to work with another student or postpone the due date until the end of the unit. You might also give them options of topics; this is often a particularly appropriate way to engage students in the writing process and to make the writing relevant to their lives. For struggling learners, sometimes we can increase their engagement by giving them supports that make assignments less threatening or scaffolds that help them work through a process independently so they get a sense of achievement. Any of these choices might increase students' engagement with a learning task and help them develop a positive outlook, or affect, about it. We will look at the engagement principle and its implementation in writing instruction in more depth in Chapter 4.

UDL Principle #2: Multiple Means of Representation

CAST calls representation the "what" of learning. From a student's perspective, that might be translated as, "*What* am I learning, and how are you going to teach it to me?" The UDL principle of representation asks the teacher to present the content in a variety of different formats; students need to see, hear, and experience the content through a range of encounters that take into account the natural learner variability that we see in every classroom (CAST, 2014).

When teachers are considering how to represent (or teach) new information, they need to bear in mind that a student's ability to understand what they are presenting is controlled by the recognition network in his brain. The recognition network is the part of the brain that is responsible for making meaning of the stimuli that we assimilate through our senses—what we see, hear, taste, smell, and touch. For example, as I am sitting at my desk writing this chapter, I hear a light tapping/rattling sound in the background. The recognition system in my brain instantly interprets this as the sound my puppy makes when she is chewing on a bone—a very familiar sound around my house! I am not looking at her, and I can't smell her near me, but I am able to take what I am hearing and make meaning of it based on my previous experiences. That is the job of the recognition network.

Dominiquechappard
https://openclipart.org/
detail/86017/what-?-
by-cybergedeon

All of us have natural strengths and weaknesses in terms of our brains' abilities to interpret stimuli through the recognition systems. My friend Sue says she learns best by sitting and listening to a lecture while taking notes. Another friend, Rachel, gets absolutely miserable if asked to sit still and listen for a long time. Obviously, their recognition systems might need different inputs in order for them both to learn to their potential. Many people claim to learn best when given visual representations of content, while others like to interact and manipulate things in order to learn. All of these modalities come under the purview of the recognition network.

STUDENT SKETCH

Imagine you are Missy. Since the first day you've been in school you've been plagued by two things: you have trouble decoding text, and you have difficulty sitting still. In fourth grade, your teacher, Mrs. Draxton, was a wonderful storyteller, and every afternoon, she would captivate you with tales of westward expansion and the California missions. Each day you would run home from school and tell your mother all about the wonderful things you were learning in social studies, and you got very excited about the reports and projects you had to complete in that class. Now you're in fifth grade, and your new teacher, Mr. Steinhouse, expects you to read the social studies book and discuss what you have read in class. Every day you sit down to try to read the assigned pages, but after a paragraph you are exhausted by the effort of trying to decode the multiple-syllable words, and soon you are twitching around in your seat and asking to go to the bathroom. Even though you are very interested in American history, you can't seem to get involved in the content, and you are often left behind in the class discussions.

For Missy, the divergent styles in which her two teachers represented the content in social studies made the difference between enthusiasm and disconnection. Was Mr. Steinhouse wrong to ask his students to independently read the text? No! But by providing only that one option for the intake of information, he was effectively cutting off the students for whom text is an ineffective means of learning. If Mr. Steinhouse had provided options for his students to listen to a digital version of the book or to read with a partner, Missy (and many other students) would have had the opportunity to receive and process the information through a modality that played to her strengths instead of her weaknesses.

INSIDER TIPS

*It's important to note that the objective of Mr. Steinhouse's lesson wasn't to practice reading skills, it was to process and discuss social studies content. So even though it's critically important for Missy to improve her decoding skills, in this case what she needed was to be able to access the information without the interference of decoding. When thinking about how to give students access to information, teachers have to **separate the goal** of the lesson **from the means** of access. If the goal of the lesson is to increase decoding skills and fluency, then the students need to read the text themselves. If the goal of the lesson is to learn about the chemical elements, then using devices that read aloud to students or having students read with a peer partner will achieve the goal and give all students access. If the goal of the lesson is to improve students' reading comprehension, teachers will have to make a* *philosophical decision about how to proceed. I would argue that students can work on their comprehension skills separately from decoding and that a student could listen to a text read aloud and get the same comprehension benefits as any other student, but for some teachers, that is a difficult concept to accept.*

UDL asks teachers to consider presenting information in a variety of contexts and media so that it can be accessed by the widest possible audience. We will look in detail at the principle of representation and its application to writing in Chapters 5 and 6.

UDL Principle #3: Multiple Means of Action/Expression

The UDL principle of action and expression is what CAST calls the *how* of learning. For a student, that might be translated as, "*How can I show you what I've learned?*" In this principle, teachers are asked to give students options for demonstrating what they know and to provide opportunities for students to develop expertise in understanding and managing their own learning (CAST, 2014). The mind map at the beginning of this chapter is a wonderful example of an *action/expression* option. Students can use mind maps to organize, display, and elaborate on new information, using graphics, words, and connecting lines to show their understanding. For many kids, a mind map can be a powerful tool for expressing what they have learned.

The strategic network of the brain directs the expression of knowledge. This network oversees the purposeful completion of tasks, including the actions that are needed to plan, execute, and follow through. We use the strategic network of our brain all day long as we undertake

our daily activities, from the automatic behaviors related to walking, eating, and reading, to the more deliberate and complex behaviors such as planning a menu, building a playhouse, or learning to speak French. Although all of these behaviors also involve elements of the affective and recognition networks, the strategic network is usually the one responsible for seeing the behaviors through to completion.

In school, students activate the strategic network to take a test, plan and write a paper, create a diorama of the three branches of government, or take notes during a lecture. Since the strategic network is implicated in such a wide range of tasks, it has specialized areas that support the development of motor skills (such as those needed to write a sentence), the planning and sequencing of behaviors (for example, the complex series of steps needed to bake a cake), and overseeing the completion of projects by monitoring and assessing progress and making corrections as needed.

STUDENT SKETCH

Erika, a young lady with cerebral palsy, is bright and motivated. She loves learning, and even more, she loves interacting with the other students in her class on learning-related projects. Erika was very excited when she found out that her class would be creating a medieval Japanese village for the seventh-grade history fair, and she looked forward to working with her classmates on the project after school. However, as they began to work on creating the village, Erika soon found that her poor fine-motor skills were hampering her participation; when she accidently knocked over a jar of paint with her elbow, one of the boys called her a klutz and told her she was just in the way. Luckily for Erika, her teacher, Ms. Schwartz, saw the interaction and came up with a plan. Recognizing that Erika had an exceptionally positive disposition and the ability to work productively with all types of personalities, Mrs. Schwartz made two quick changes. First, she gave Erika a bingo dauber filled with paint that allowed her to paint large areas without fear of spilling. Second, she made Erika the foreperson of the project and put her in charge of managing and organizing the construction. Thanks to Mrs. Schwartz's insight into her strengths, Erika worked with her peers to create a construction plan, assigned students to different parts of the construction, participated in painting the sets, and directed the project through to completion, earning the gratitude and respect of her classmates.

In order to follow through on a learning task, students need to know how to take advantage of their own learning strengths to show what they know. They have to set learning goals, strategize the steps needed to complete them, and purposefully work their way through those steps. The principle of action and expression helps teachers support their students in the development of these skills while giving them options that allow them to express their learning by leveraging their areas of strength. We will closely examine this principle and its relationship to writing in Chapter 7.

WHY NOW?

If you are like me, every time you hear about another initiative or "innovation" in education, you may feel a little skeptical. Many times it feels like we are giving teachers one more thing to do in the classroom and that it isn't worth the effort to invest time and energy in a new idea that will eventually fade from the educational scene.

I want to assure you: UDL is not "just one more thing" that teachers have to do. It's not a top-down mandate created by people who haven't set foot in a classroom for decades. It's an educational framework carefully developed and fine-tuned in classrooms for more than thirty years that works in partnership with other educational reforms to make the curriculum responsive to individual student needs while reducing the need for extensive accommodations (Meyer, Rose, & Gordon, 2014). It is a set of tools that can improve any lesson and that, if implemented thoughtfully and proactively, can actually make the teacher's job *easier.*

Additionally, the ideas behind UDL are not new; as long ago as the mid-1900s, the groundbreaking educator Lev Vygotsky proposed a profound and fundamental relationship between three elements in the classroom: the environment, the teacher, and the student (Liu & Matthews, 2005). These three elements form the foundation for the three principles of UDL: engagement (the interaction between the student and the environment), representation (the interaction between the teacher and the student), and action/expression (the interaction between the student and the curriculum). The creators of UDL aren't proposing anything new, they are offering a new perspective on the interactions of these three primary elements and a framework through which teachers can make the curriculum more effective for all their learners.

Author and public speaker Sir Ken Robinson, in his lecture "How to Escape Education's Death Valley," proposed the following:

> We have to go from what is essentially an industrial model of education, a manufacturing model, which is based on linearity and conformity and batching people. We have to move to a model that is based more on principles of agriculture. We have to recognize that human flourishing is not a mechanical process; it's an organic process. And you cannot predict the outcome of human development. All you can do, like a farmer, is create the conditions under which they will begin to flourish. (TED Talks, 2013)

UDL helps teachers create conditions in which children can flourish; UDL proposes that if children aren't learning the way we are teaching, we should teach the way they learn.

WRAPPING UP THE BIG IDEAS

- UDL lessons are designed from the beginning to be flexible and responsive to learner variability.
- When we teach to the middle, we are designing our lessons for a mythical "average learner" that provides an ill-fitting education to most students.
- We can create "disabled learners" by designing curricula that doesn't acknowledge that students differ in the ways they learn and function in the classroom.
- The principle of engagement asks us to create a classroom that motivates and engages our students in the learning tasks. Engagement is regulated by the affective system in the brain.
- The principle of representation asks us to deliver instruction in a variety of ways to take into account the natural variability of the learners in our classrooms. This principle is built around the recognition system of the brain, which takes in and interprets sensory information.
- The principle of action/expression asks us to give students options to show us what they've learned. It is designed around the strategic network of the brain, which directs the expression of knowledge.
- UDL is a framework for delivering instruction, not "one more thing" teachers have to do.

[handwritten margin notes: enviro, teacher, student]

FOR FURTHER READING

Hall, T., Strangman, N., & Meyer, A. (2011). *Differentiated instruction and implications for UDL implementation* (National Center on Accessing the General Curriculum Report). Retrieved from http://www.cast.org/system/galleries/download/ncac/DI_UDL.pdf

Meyer, A., Rose, D. H., & Gordon, D. (2014). *Universal Design for Learning: Theory and practice.* Wakefield, MA: CAST.

Rose, D. H., & Gravel, J. W. (2009). Getting from here to there: UDL, global positioning systems, and lessons for improving education. In D. T. Gordon, J. W. Gravel, & L. A. Schifter (Eds.), *A policy reader in Universal Design for Learning* (pp. 5–18). Cambridge, MA: Harvard Education Press.

Engagement

4

If students aren't interested, they won't learn.
If students aren't paying attention, they won't learn.
If students aren't motivated, they won't learn.
ENGAGEMENT IS EVERYTHING.

The principle of engagement is sometimes one of the hardest UDL principles for teachers to understand. Until recently, it was listed as the third principle on the UDL guideline sheet, but in the 2014 update, the Center for Applied Special Technology (CAST) moved engagement to the first position. Even though there is no order to the UDL principles per se, they realized, as Nancy and I do, that engagement affects *everything* we do in the classroom. Or as we've conceptualized it in the UDL VennBrella, it's the canopy that encompasses and shelters the other two principles, allowing them to work effectively in the classroom.

In our vision of UDL, *engagement* is an overarching philosophy or culture that has a constant impact on the other two principles. Without engagement, students are unlikely to be motivated or interested in the curriculum. So no matter how you represent the material and no matter how the students express their learning, the classroom may not be productive.

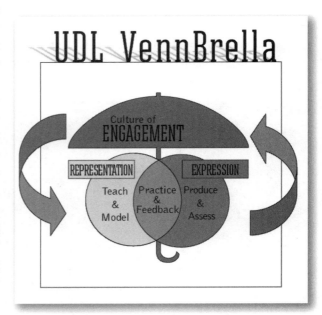

However, this isn't a one-way model. The arrows represent the interactive, symbiotic nature of the relationship between the elements. The methods a teacher chooses to represent the curriculum and the options she gives the students for expression will both have a strong reciprocal impact on student engagement. Nevertheless, we feel that the culture a teacher creates in the classroom impacts everything else that happens, and teachers who create a culture of engagement provide the optimum atmosphere for student growth and achievement.

THE CULTURE OF ENGAGEMENT

The Merriam-Webster online dictionary (www.merriam-webster.com) defines culture as the following:

- **The beliefs, customs, arts, etc., of a particular society, group, place, or time**
- **A way of thinking, behaving, or working that exists in a place or organization (such as a business)**

I think this is a perfect definition of a classroom. As a teacher, you have educational beliefs, customs, and behaviors, many of which may have come from the classrooms in which you grew up. You use these beliefs to create your own classroom culture and to shape the ways of thinking and behaving of your students.

Consider this picture.

In the 1950s and '60s, this was probably considered the ideal classroom. The decidedly nondiverse children were sitting quietly in rows and

[photo source to come]

were expected to work individually on paper-and-pencil tasks. The classroom was most likely extremely quiet, and the students who finished their work would not get out a book or work on another project; they would put down their pencils, fold their hands on their desks, and sit silently facing forward. The culture of that classroom most likely valued "traditional" school behaviors, such as being the first one finished, being the first to know the answer, and the memorization of facts. The students were in competition with each other to be the best behaved and the smartest, and the teacher was queen, sitting at the front of the classroom "pouring" information into the empty vessels that were her quiet, compliant students.

Very few of us value that type of classroom today, but remnants of that "ideal" classroom still linger in the memories of many teachers. What does the ideal, engaging classroom look like today? The truth is, an engaging classroom can be difficult to define, and what's engaging to one student can be quite the opposite to another.

Take a look at these examples:

This is Jenna. Jenna loves to learn by listening. She has really strong auditory memory and enjoys listening to teachers tell stories and lecture about topics of interest. She is also shy, so she hates when she is required to work with her peers or to give her opinion in class. For her, the engaging classroom is teacher-centered and structured.

Meet Eric. He is very social and is quite popular with his peers. His idea of an engaging classroom is one in which he gets lots of opportunities to work with his friends, interacting around assignments or projects. He doesn't enjoy sitting still and listening, so he often tunes out during lectures and teacher-led activities.

Say hello to Katie. Katie is a highly active individual. She excels in sports and runs five miles every day after school. When she was in second grade, her teacher used to sit her in the back of the class so she could stand up, walk around, or bounce on an exercise ball during class. Katie's idea of an engaging classroom is one where she gets to build things, act things out, or work with her hands. She likes anything that gets her moving!

This is Amir. Amir is a skilled learner who loves to dig deeply into topics and explore on his own. Although he doesn't have trouble listening in the classroom, he quickly gets bored and his mind moves on to new things. He loves research projects and likes to be challenged. His idea of an engaging classroom is one in which he is given a computer or tablet and assigned a learning task to complete independently. Group projects frustrate him.

As you can see, the prospect of creating the ideal classroom culture for this group of students is daunting. The work that makes Amir happiest is likely to bore and possibly frustrate many of the other students. Jenna's learning preference is highly aversive to Katie and Eric. What is a teacher to do?

PROVIDING STUDENTS WITH OPTIONS

©Mark Heeter. http://usarmy.vo.llnwd.net/e2/-images/2009/10/13/52864

The idea of student options becomes very important as we consider the highly diverse learning preferences of the students in the classroom above. To make it even more challenging, as we explored in Chapter 1, writing is inherently difficult for many kids. So if they aren't engaged and motivated to write, they won't be able to get beyond the stringent demands inherent in the task. For struggling writers, engagement is even more important, and creating a culture of engagement becomes a critical component of any classroom devoted to building writing skills for all learners.

So what exactly is a culture of engagement? Well, if we go back to our definition of culture, a culture of engagement should include beliefs, customs, and ways of behaving that encourage student involvement. A teacher who builds a culture of engagement creates a classroom that **values choice** and **empowers students as learners**. A culture of engagement helps students become **knowledgeable about their own learning strengths** and gives them **options about how to implement them**. In the culture of engagement, students are **active participants** in the learning process, with opportunities to **learn from and with one another** and with the understanding that there is **no one way of learning** that works for all kids (CAST, 2014).

Going back to our VennBrella, a culture of engagement might look like the illustration on page 43.

All of these elements working together in the classroom create an atmosphere of student empowerment and involvement that we call "The Culture of Engagement." Let's take a look at some of these elements in more detail now.

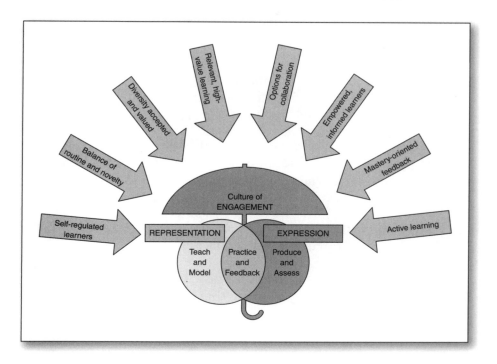

Your Learning Options

In the spirit of UDL choice, we are going to give you several options for how to learn about the big ideas in the next four chapters. If you are a person who likes to learn by listening, go to http://resources .corwin.com/spencerudl and click on *podcasts* to hear Nancy explain the big ideas of each chapter to you in her very best engaging manner. If you are a person who would prefer to see those ideas displayed as a graphic, click on *slideshows* at the same link to see the big ideas laid out for you in a visual format. If you are an independent learner who really prefers to explore concepts on your own, go to the website of the National Center on Universal Design for Learning where you can browse to your heart's content. The pages on each of the principles of UDL can be accessed from this link: http://www.udlcenter.org/aboutudl/udlguidelines. Finally, if you are a person who learns best by reading, I encourage you to read the big ideas presented in the boxes at the end of every chapter. We like to think we are offering you a smorgasbord of learning options, so please taste all the items that appeal to you, and think about how you can offer similar options to the students in your class.

CAST presents three guidelines for creating engagement in the classroom:

Options for self-regulation. In this guideline, students become expert learners by identifying their learning strengths and preferences, as well as the tools that help them learn to their maximum potential.

Options for sustaining effort and persistence. Under this guideline, the teacher helps students master strategies for persevering in the face of difficult tasks and long-term projects.

Options for recruiting interest. This guideline is designed to increase student engagement through relevant, authentic work and the reduction of threat and distraction.

We will look at these guidelines next and discuss strategies for creating a culture of engagement that will help your struggling writers succeed.

GUIDELINE #1: SELF-REGULATION

One of the most important skills we can teach a student is how to regulate his or her own academic and behavioral functioning. Students need to learn about themselves as learners and as individuals, and they need to recognize and appreciate their strengths so they may leverage them to overcome their challenges. Students also need to manage the rules of the classroom and adapt to the varied expectations of different teachers. CAST tells us this: "Unfortunately some classrooms do not address these skills explicitly, leaving them as part of the 'implicit' curriculum that is often inaccessible or invisible to many."

The *hidden curriculum* is the name given to the unspoken expectations, rules, and values in schools and classrooms. Rick Lavoie, author and host of the classic "FAT City" video, has talked for years about the hidden curriculum's effect on students with disabilities, but the truth is that it isn't just students with disabilities who sometimes fail to pick up on the implicit expectations in a classroom (Lavoie & Levine, 2005). Many students struggle to learn the tacit rules of teachers and schools, and the teacher who spends time making these expectations explicit will find himself with students who are better able to function in the classroom. Table 4.1 offers some of the elements of the hidden curriculum that can be particularly problematic during writing instruction.

Table 4.1 Elements of the Hidden Curriculum in Writing Instruction

Implicit Expectations	The Trap	What Teachers Can Do
Students should always follow the rules.	The rules vary from classroom to classroom, school to school, teacher to teacher, and subject to subject. The rules for independent work time (which often includes writing) can be particularly confusing for some students.	Explicitly teach and practice the classroom expectations for writing time, and give reminders often. (Remember, some students struggle with memory deficits that can impact this significantly!) Consider using private prompts and reminders where needed.
There are appropriate and inappropriate ways to ask for help.	Many kids have difficulty interpreting the social cues that should tell them that the teacher is busy and they should wait to ask for help. Children with this issue are often confused and discouraged by the teachers' responses, not understanding what they "did wrong." This comes up often in writing, where students sometimes need specific and frequent feedback from the teacher.	Cue the student to be aware of the social cues that s/he is missing, for example: "What are some things you can do while you wait for me to be free?" Use visual systems to "get students in line" for help, such as clothespins on a sentence strip. When they need help, students put their clip on the strip, then wait in their desks until their name is called.
You have to manage your time and transition to a new activity when time is up.	For some students, transitioning from one activity to another is very problematic. Meltdowns happen when they aren't aware of the time or when they aren't done with whatever they are doing. In writer's workshop, students are often asked to stop before their work is complete, so this can trigger problems.	Give *frequent* reminders when transitions are coming up. "We will stop writing in five (two . . . one) minutes." Give private prompts to students who struggle with transitions. "Sadie, when you finish the sentence you're writing, start to put your materials away." Assign peer buddies to remind each other of appropriate transition behaviors.

(Continued)

Table 4.1 (Continued)

Implicit Expectations	The Trap	What Teachers Can Do
When the teacher is talking, your job is to sit quietly and listen.	Some students have trouble discriminating when it is okay to get up and sharpen a pencil or get a drink and when it is not. They don't take in the cues of the other students around them and the general atmosphere of the classroom during instruction.	Provide gentle reminders as needed. If some students are really having difficulty, consider using a visual cue such as a sign or stoplight (see Figure 4.1). If a student still responds inappropriately, *don't* tell him the behavior you expect. Point to the visual cue to help him process and remember on his own.
Be supportive during peer editing.	The expectations for giving and receiving feedback can be confusing to many students. This is as true in high school as it is in first grade.	Explicitly teach students how to give supportive feedback and how to use a rubric to guide editing conversations. Model how to talk to a partner who may have hurt your feelings and how to get assistance from the teacher when intervention is needed.

Figure 4.1 The Classroom Stoplight

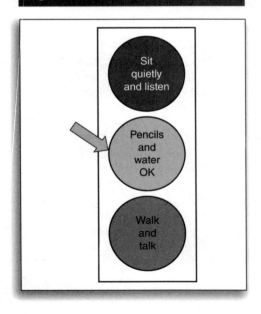

There are many more social and cultural norms that are part of the hidden curriculum in schools, but the manner for dealing with them remains the same.

1. Don't punish or embarrass a child who makes a mistake with these implied rules.

2. Don't assume that a child understands the expectations.

3. Explicitly teach the hidden skills a student needs to be successful.

4. Provide opportunities for practice and feedback.

5. Provide visual aids and prompts to guide all the students.

Teaching Personal Coping Skills in Writing

Because of the high-level physical and cognitive demands of writing, students will frequently get discouraged. Teachers, with their big hearts, will rush to their aid, talking them through the problem and guiding them toward mastery of the task. Although this is done with the best intentions, for some students this is a path toward learned helplessness.

Learned helplessness is what happens when students discover, "Hey! If I don't try very hard, someone will usually come over and help me!" Unfortunately, because writing is such a difficult subject for so many of our students, learned helplessness is a particular problem among struggling writers. In their efforts to support these students, well-meaning teachers frequently *over*-support them, unwittingly teaching them that the only way they can write successfully is if someone gives them help.

Technology is an important tool for helping struggling writers develop self-sufficiency and avoid learned helplessness. However, using technology as a tool for written expression is a skill unto itself; you can't just hand a young person an iPad and assume that she will be able to use it to dictate an essay. Moreover, different technology applications will work for different students. Some students will easily learn to dictate and edit text, whereas for others, that will not be an effective tool. Some students will love word-prediction software, and for others, it will be an exercise in frustration. Some will be most effective if simply allowed to do all their writing on a keyboard. But whatever technology students ultimately choose, they need to be provided with scaffolded instruction and practice in order to use it effectively. Below are some of the options you should consider providing in your classroom.

Speech-to-Text Devices

Speech-to-text devices have become ubiquitous in today's world; many if not most of us carry one in our pocket in the form of a smartphone. Siri, perhaps the most well known of the new speech-to-text applications, provided a breakthrough in the accuracy of speech to text and is a tool that is now available and accessible for a wide variety of learners. Dragon Dictate,
long a classroom staple in special education, is also now available as an app for smartphones and tablets and is a well-proven tool for students who can benefit from the opportunity to dictate text. New speech-to-text apps come out daily in both iOS and Android formats, and the opportunities for students to dictate their writing become broader all the time.

Teaching a student to use a speech-to-text device can create self-sufficiency and lower frustration in students who are held back in their writing due to poor motor functioning, poor spelling, or individuals with a temporary disabling condition such as a sprained wrist. It can also be useful for students whose brains work faster than their pens—those rapid thinking, creative young people who need to get their thoughts on the paper as quickly as possible before going back and editing. Of course, many other learners can also benefit from and enjoy the opportunity to use speech-to-text technology.

When should we use it? When you're considering whether to let your students dictate their writing instead of writing it by hand, you need to separate the *goal* of the instruction from the *means* of obtaining the goal. If your instructional goal is for students to practice their cursive handwriting, then obviously this is a poor time to consider speech to text. However, if your instructional goal is for students to develop a well-organized, well-supported paragraph or essay, then speech to text is a tool that will help many learners.

How should we teach it? Like many other technology applications, speech to text requires experimentation and practice and will work differently for different students. The first step is to let them explore freely, just getting used to the device. Once they understand a little bit about how it functions, teachers should begin to model how to use it for writing, scaffolding the students' basic skills with the tool. Once they have mastered the basics, students can experiment with different ways to use it in their writing and figure out what works best for them.

In order for students to be successful with speech-to-text devices, their use needs to be explicitly taught and practiced. Consider using the following steps to help your students become proficient with speech-to-text tools.

1) ***Model and practice spoken punctuation.*** *Before students can begin to write using speech to text, they need to practice saying punctuation out loud. For example, if a student wants to write "**The dog ran up the hill,**" he has to say "**The dog ran up the hill period.**" For a speech-to-text application to work effectively, the punctuation has to be said aloud. This is an acquired skill but one that many students can master, at least at the level of ending punctuation such as periods and question marks. Teachers should model not only the dictation process but also the use of verbal punctuation. If a student still cannot verbalize ending punctuation after plenty of practice, another option is to dictate one sentence at a time. Students can dictate a sentence, stop the dictation, then add the punctuation. Then they dictate the next sentence, stop dictation, add punctuation, and so on.*

2) ***Teach basic editing.*** *Once students have mastered the process of dictating one or two simple sentences with ending punctuation, they also need to practice the editing process. Teachers should scaffold this process by beginning with short, simple sentences, gradually working up to brief paragraphs. Give students the opportunity to practice replacing vocabulary, adding commas and other punctuation, and moving text around.* ***These basic skills should be mastered before the student ever tries to do any authentic writing with the technology.***

Like any other skill, students will need a lot of practice and guidance to master the use of speech-to-text technology, but for some it can ultimately be the key to independence. As noted earlier, many students now have a speech-to-text device in their pocket at all times, and allowing them to use it as a tool for writing goes a long way toward creating a culture of engagement during writing instruction.

STUDENT SKETCH

Reynaldo, a ninth grader, has the ability to think about topics and generate ideas just like any other ninth grader; in fact, he is an engaged and articulate student during classroom discussions. Unfortunately, Reynaldo has extreme deficits in spelling and fine-motor skills that seriously hamper his ability to produce written work. When he was in elementary school, his classrooms had very limited technology, and Reynaldo was not offered other options to help him get his ideas on paper. As a result, he never discovered his own aptitude for composing text. When he arrived at high school, however, his teacher gave him the opportunity to try out different tools and technologies to discover which ones helped him unlock his writing potential. Voilà! With the help of a speech-to-text program, Reynaldo soon discovered that he had the heart of an author, and before long he was turning out multiple-page stories and essays that were a joy to read. For Reynaldo, and many students like him, learning to use technology and exploring different options for getting his ideas on paper was an important part of learning about his own strengths as a writer and, thus, a critical component of the culture of engagement.

Word-Prediction Software

Word-prediction software is a specialized adaptive tool that helps students for whom speech to text is not a viable option. With word-prediction software, the student types his text, but as he types, a pop-up box appears at the bottom of the page with words for him to choose from. For example, if he typed the letters *co*, the software might give him *could, cold, come*, and several other words beginning with the letters *co*. Predictions are made using syntax as well as taking into account the most commonly used words in everyday English. The student has the options to continue typing or to choose one of the words to go in his document.

Word-prediction software has traditionally required some specialized training, and most students spend some time with an occupational therapist or some other specialist in order to learn the software. However, the latest versions of some texting apps on smartphones include word prediction, so for many young people it is not the mystery it once was. Co-Writer, from Don Johnson Incorporated, is probably the best known of the word-prediction software programs, but other available options include Aurora Suite, SpeakQ, and WordQ.

The iReadWrite app for iPad, although not cheap, provides an extraordinary number of writing tools in one application. It includes contextual word prediction, text to speech (a read-aloud feature), spell check, confusable word checker, a picture-and-word dictionary, and customizable backgrounds, fonts, and voices to assist even those writers who need the most support.

Developing Metacognition

Metacognition is the understanding of one's own thinking; some people call it "learning how to learn." Many typical students begin to understand themselves as learners gradually over time, by gaining an appreciation of what they do well in the classroom. This can be much more difficult, however, if you are a student whose learning patterns fall outside the classroom norms. You may never have the opportunity to identify your learning strengths if you don't get to "try them out" at school.

IMAGINE THIS . . .

You are the child of two renowned symphony musicians, both of whom have long family histories of musical prodigy. When you are one year old, you are shipwrecked on a desert island with a society of people who have no music. For the next fifteen years of your life you live happily without music, developing skills in cooking, weaving, and farming. At the age of sixteen, you are rescued and taken back to your family. Your parents are horrified to discover that you have absolutely no understanding or affinity for music. You don't understand rhythm, you know nothing of melody or intonation—you have absolutely no sense of yourself as a musical being. Because your inherited aptitude for music fell outside of the norms of the island culture, you never had the chance to develop it; if you had to take a test to measure your musical ability, you would fail.

The previous scenario is very much like the experience of some children with learning differences in non-UDL classrooms. When a classroom has a very narrow window of accepted academic behavior, a child whose academic strengths fall outside of that window is unlikely to discover what he can do well. Just like that child who was never exposed to music, a nontypical learner may have absolutely no sense of his own intrinsic academic potential.

Mastery-Oriented Feedback. One of the most important things teachers can do to increase metacognitive awareness in struggling learners is help them learn to appreciate their own strengths. One way to do this is to provide mastery-oriented feedback to your students. Mastery-oriented feedback is feedback that is focused on progress rather than an "ideal," or rather than comparing one student's work to another's (CAST, 2012). It takes the focus off of inherent ability and instead puts it on students' effort, persistence, and growth. Mastery-oriented feedback helps students stop thinking of themselves as "smart" or "not smart," and instead helps them realize that, with practice, they can make progress through their own efforts. Figure 4.2 shows CAST's recommendations for feedback that will help students develop metacognition.

Figure 4.2   Mastery-Oriented Feedback

1. Provide feedback that is focused on effort and persistence. Even if a student's work isn't yet where you would like it to be, reward and praise hard work.

2. Help students learn to identify and appreciate what they do well. It's one thing for the teacher to tell a student what's good about her work, but in order for her to develop metacognition she needs to learn to identify it herself. Use cues to help students identify their strengths, such as, "I particularly like something you've done in this sentence—do you know what it is?" or "What do you think about your use of adjectives in this paragraph?"

3. Use rubrics to provide a concrete standard for students' writing. Not all students will be able to achieve the same standard, so identifying specific targets in the rubric for each student can give each student an achievable goal.

4. Make your feedback frequent and timely; the more specific and focused it can be, the better. Feedback such as "You really worked hard on this—it's much better!" is not as helpful as "I can really see where you went back and improved the vocabulary in this passage. Your word choice is much improved!"

5. Use questions to guide students to identifying their own areas for improvement. Metacognition includes knowing your strengths as well as being able to independently identify areas for improvement.

Source: CAST (2012).

Mr. Kennedy was working at a kidney table with a small group of students, all of whom were editing a draft of their writing. A young student named Dalia put down her pencil and handed her paper to Mr. Kennedy. He read over her paragraph, then looked up at her with a smile and said, "This is beautiful work, Dalia! I'm really proud of you!"

Obviously, this feedback made Dalia feel very good. Unfortunately, Dalia is a struggling learner and does not have a good awareness of her own strengths. She had no idea what she had done that pleased Mr. Kennedy. Even though the feedback was positive and made Dalia feel wonderful, it was not very useful to her, and it was definitely not useful to the other students working at the table. They had no idea what Dalia had done to earn Mr. Kennedy's praise.

Imagine if Mr. Kennedy had said this instead. "Dalia, this is really beautiful work. You've done something here that really good writers do. You have edited your paragraph so that there are many different kinds of sentences in it, which makes it very interesting to read. That is something really good writers do. I'm super proud of you." Now, Dalia feels like queen of the world. She knows what she did to earn the positive feedback, and you can be sure that she will keep doing it so she can keep getting the praise. Equally important, however, is the fact that the other students also now know what Dalia did, and because they would also like to get positive feedback from their teacher, they are going to make an effort to imitate her behavior. By giving very specific feedback, Mr. Kennedy is improving the learning of all his students.

Specificity is an important part of mastery-oriented feedback. Equally important is feedback that is focused on effort and that helps students understand their own learning. In Dalia's case, Mr. Kennedy might have added a statement such as, "I know it took a lot of effort to do this, and I saw how many times you worked through your paragraph. It really paid off. Maybe you can help others in the group figure out how to vary the sentence structure in their paragraphs." Now Mr. Kennedy has helped Dalia and the other students focus on the *process* of creating good writing rather than just the outcome. The emphasis is on student effort, and his feedback clearly guides students to maximize their own efforts as they edit. By providing Dalia with the opportunity to help other students, he has recognized her acquisition of the skills and moved her one step closer to mastery of this skill.

GUIDELINE #2: SUSTAINING EFFORT

The second UDL guideline for engagement is providing options for sustaining effort and persistence. The ability to work hard, even on very difficult tasks, is a skill that even many adults have not mastered, but is one that can make a lifelong difference for any child.

Varying Classroom Demands

One of the important principles of this UDL guideline is the recognition that not all students like the same type of classroom procedures. Some students (and many adults) are most comfortable with predictability and will function most effectively when they clearly understand what happens next. For other students, that lack of variation is really boring and leads to off-task behaviors and acting out in an effort to disrupt the sameness.

Classroom guru Spencer Kagan proposes that if a classroom culture depends mostly on routine, with very little novelty, many students will be bored, which causes stress. Similarly, if a classroom is all novelty with very little routine, students can also be stressed (Kagan & Kagan, 2009). He recommends that teachers seek to balance routine and novelty, so that students at both ends of the spectrum are comfortable. Kagan uses a graphic like the one in Figure 4.3 to represent the options.

Allow students to choose the level of novelty. What does it really mean to provide a balance of novelty and routine? That "balance" might look very different from the perspectives of different types of students; for example, many students with autism can be overwhelmed by even small amounts of novelty. Given the varied preferences of our student population, UDL

Figure 4.3

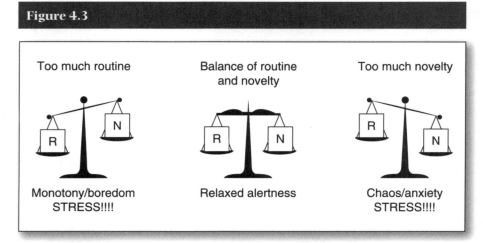

Adapted from Kagan & Kagan, 2009.

recommends providing options for students so that, whenever possible, they can *choose* the level of novelty that suits them at any given moment on any particular task. For example, if Jonathan is feeling overwhelmed today, he might pick the option of completing a worksheet in a familiar format, rather than tackling a new project or working on a group assignment. On another day Jonathan might choose a completely different option. He is able to pick the level of novelty that works best given his state of mind each day.

Create a menu of options. Some teachers like to create a menu of options—I have seen this used very successfully in classrooms from about second grade on up. The "structured options" built into the menu can be successful in making every student feel more comfortable, including those who like routine and those who prefer novelty. Even though all the students have the same work to complete, the menus give them choices about what to complete next and when to complete it. For a child who has difficulty sustaining effort, having the choice of when to complete aversive activities can be empowering. I think about a fifth-grade student I knew, Stanley, who hated math and had a meltdown every time he was given math work to complete. Stan's teacher gave him a menu of options and allowed him to choose when in the day he would do his math pages. Completing ten minutes of math at a time, broken up by other work that he found less objectionable, allowed Stanley to get the required work done without the frequent meltdowns that had previously plagued his teacher.

An elementary menu might look like the one below. Included in it are all the independent work activities that the students need to complete during the week. The student has the option to look at the menu, pick the activity that she wants to work on next, and the next time she has some free work time, she picks another activity. For students who have particular trouble completing a certain type of task, like Stanley, teachers might "weight" the assignments with different point values in order to increase motivation.

Measurement Activity	Math Practice	Spelling Practice
Writer's Workshop	Reading Practice	Free Reading
iPad Activities	Multiplication Facts	Social Studies Project

For secondary students working on writing, a teacher could create a menu of options around writing subskills, still providing students choices about what to practice. The following activities are all taken from the CCSS on writing and language, Grade 8. Students might have the option to work on blogging on an iPad, work with figurative language, or complete storyboards (among other things) during their writing free-choice time.

Concluding Statements	Active and Passive Verbs	Using Transitions
Storyboarding	Vocabulary Work	Gathering and Assessing Evidence
iPad Blogging	Figures of Speech	Research Project

Another simple but highly effective low-tech option for helping students sustain effort is providing them with choices of writing instruments. As silly as it sounds, the right pencil or pen can also make all the difference in the world to a student who hates to write. I know high school teachers who keep a variety of silly pens and pencils available to their students; some teachers swear by the motivational power of these funny writing instruments! I've seen vegetable pens, reindeer pens, lipstick pens, pens with games on the end . . . any of which can become a silly motivator for a student who doesn't feel like writing!

GUIDELINE #3: RECRUITING STUDENT INTEREST

I said it at the start of this chapter, and I'll say it again: *If students aren't paying attention, they won't learn!* It is incumbent on teachers to find ways to get all their students interested in the content they teach, but this is particularly important when you are considering students with disabilities and/or learning challenges. They *must* be focused and attending to instruction or they are unlikely to learn. As a result, this third UDL guideline, recruiting student interest, becomes exceptionally important when we are hoping to teach writing to this particular population of students.

Providing Choice and Autonomy

One of the defining characteristics of UDL, which is interwoven throughout all of the guidelines, is this idea of providing students with options or choices. In fact, if I had to boil UDL down into one word, I would probably identify the concept of *options* as the most important big idea of UDL. Options empower students, build motivation, and help them become expert learners in their own unique ways. Each of the nine UDL guidelines, as originally defined by CAST, is created as a series of options. This one, for example, is written on the CAST website as, "Provide options for recruiting interest." UDL is all about providing the students with choices.

These choices can take on a variety of faces in the classroom. You can give students choices about where to sit as they complete their work, what tools to use (pen vs. computer vs. iPad), and what color of paper to print on. Some of these choices are relatively simple, and most teachers integrate them naturally. On the other hand, I have met teachers who believe that allowing one student to type an essay while others are handwriting gives an unfair advantage. And I would agree—having one student do something different can give the impression of favoritism and definitely can be stigmatizing to that particular student. That's why UDL asks us to provide those options to *all* our students. Most learners will sometimes choose to write by hand and sometimes choose technology, but for others, the choice to use technology can be the difference between engagement and despair. For those students, writing by hand is a "disabling" factor that keeps them from working up to their potential.

*Many teachers keep cardboard study carrels in their classrooms and use them to help focus students who are easily distracted by their environment. However, the **method** you choose to use the study carrels can have a big impact on the culture of your classroom and can serve either as punishment or as an option for developing metacognition.*

*In Mrs. Lingard's fourth-grade class, she has several desks set up on the edges of the room with study carrels on them, which she calls "the office." Students have to ask permission to work in an office, and it is considered a privilege. When a student is persistently having trouble focusing, Mrs. Lingard will schedule a private conference with him and discuss the option of working in an office when he is struggling to concentrate. After the conference, if the student is having trouble focusing during class time, she will quietly cue him to consider going to an office. **Importantly, she never forces him but instead allows him to make the choice on his own.** Over time, most of her students learn to identify when they are having trouble paying attention to their work and will voluntarily ask to move to an office. By giving the students options to work in different spaces, Mrs. Lingard has increased their metacognition about the work conditions that are most effective for them.*

Adjusting the level of challenge. We also need to provide choices about the level of challenge a student faces on a particular task. For example, it is not uncommon for fifth-grade teachers to ask every student to complete five paragraphs for practically every writing assignment—the five-paragraph essay was, until Common Core, a staple of fourth- and fifth-grade language arts standards. For a student who hates to write, however, the prospect of the five-paragraph essay is very daunting, and facing it over and over is discouraging to say the least.

A teacher can increase a student's engagement in writing simply by giving students some options about how much to write on any given topic or assignment. Sure, every student needs to learn to write a good five (or four, or seven!) paragraph essay, but not for every assignment. Imagine if every time you had to do a report card, your administrator required you to write a full-page summary for each student in each subject. You would quickly grow to dread report cards. The same holds true in writing instruction. You need to mix up the expectations for the length of writing assignments in order to hold the interest of the students in your classes for whom writing is *not* a naturally engaging subject.

STUDENT SKETCH

Jeffrey, whom I quoted at the end of Chapter 1, absolutely hated to write. As a new teacher, I was at my wit's end to persuade him to get any ideas on paper. Every time the class had a writing assignment, Jeffrey would begin to misbehave, and soon he would be pulling the whole class off task with his antics. It was almost impossible for me to get him to write a full paragraph, much less multiple paragraphs. However, Jeffrey had a very strong sense of competition, and anything that could be framed as a "challenge" automatically had much stronger appeal to him. So Jeffrey and I made a deal: for a week, when the class was working on writing projects, he only had to complete one sentence. If he sat down, wrote and edited one strong sentence, he was done with writing for the day and could move on to other things. The following week I challenged him again: I bet him that he could write and edit two really great sentences. I told him that if he could do it, he could stop writing for the day, and he could have five minutes of computer time as a reward.

You can see where this is going. . . . Soon Jeffrey was writing multiple sentences, and over time, multiple paragraphs, and reveling in his own accomplishments. It turned out that once I adjusted the expectations for him and let him experience success in this very difficult subject, over time his confidence grew, and his motivation to write grew with it.

Provide choice of topics. It is a pretty common classroom practice to allow students choices of topics on which to write, but I feel it is worth reiterating in this section. CAST emphasizes that students are engaged by activities that authentically relate to their lives and have meaning to them on a personal level. Topics that are culturally relevant to students, topics of social or political interest, and age-appropriate topics are most engaging to students and can turn reluctant writers into motivated ones. In many UDL classrooms, the students are allowed to choose topics to write about when they are working on building skills (such as practicing parenthetical phrases [L.6.2.A] or developing concluding statements [W.9-10.1.E]), but then they are assigned topics, or provided a narrow choice of topics, for other specific writing assignments, such as writing an opinion piece (W.3.1). Wherever possible, give your students options about the topics during writing instruction for maximum student engagement.

Consider choice of rewards. Different "rewards" also appeal to different students. Most teachers, even up into high school, post examples of student work on the wall, with the assumption that students are happy and proud to see it there. However, for some students, the prospect of having their work publicly displayed has the opposite effect—they are ashamed or embarrassed. That student, however, might really enjoy the opportunity to read her essay to her old second-grade teacher, to post it to Edmodo, or to videotape herself reading it to show to mom at home. UDL urges us not to assume that students are motivated by the same opportunities to display or "publish" their work and to offer options and choices instead (CAST, 2014).

Creating Relevance, Value, and Authenticity

There's no way around it—students are more engaged when schoolwork is meaningful to them. Whether it's the content being taught or the ways in which they interact with that content, if students understand how it will impact their lives, careers, or interests, they are likely to be much more engaged and motivated. In terms of writing, the CCSS made this a little easier for us when they included Writing Standard 10: writing for a range of purposes, tasks, and audiences. This standard recognizes that in college and careers, young adults will be asked to do a variety of different types of writing tasks that demand different styles and different voices. Beginning in Grade 3, students are asked to "write routinely" in both short and extended time frames and to do so for "a range of tasks, purposes and audiences." This standard remains the same from Grade 3 to 12 and provides teachers with an important framework to facilitate student choice in writing.

From a practical standpoint, how will Standard 10 play out in a UDL classroom to help increase student engagement? **Students will be involved in a wide variety of authentic writing tasks, including**

letter writing, newsletters, bulletins, opinion pieces, blogs, websites, social media, and texts. Right off the bat you can see how the demands of these different types of writing are quite diverse—a student who is blogging may be writing in a radically different voice than one who is writing an opinion piece, for example. A blog post might be one paragraph, while an opinion piece might be three pages. The key here is empowering the students to make some choices about which tool and outlet they are going to use for different assignments.

Let's get even more specific. Table 4.2 shows you a few of the ways UDL can interact with the CCSS to provide students with options related to the CCSS writing standards. I've provided activities at a variety of grade levels and for different standards, and since the standards are spiralled through the grade levels, most of these can also be adapted for different ages of students and different applications. The goal is twofold: provide students with choices about how they can fulfill the writing requirements of the CCSS, and give them options that encourage their creativity. These choices will motivate your students and give them the opportunity to play to their strengths as they develop their writing skills. In addition, each of these options requires a different style and amount of writing, which will help your struggling writers meet the CCSS writing expectations.

Reducing Threats

This always sound so ominous to me—reducing threats?!? What kind of "threats" could there be in a classroom? Well, as dramatic as it sounds, threat is an ongoing part of classroom life for students with learning challenges. I'd like to tell you a story about my former student, Jake.

Jake was a young man with a learning disability. He was sharp as a tack and very personable, but he struggled to read. Jake was a witty, likable young man who had plenty of friends, and by the end of every school year, he would be comfortably ensconced in the culture of his classroom. Everyone understood his unique intelligence, and he was appreciated and respected by his classmates.

TEACHER'S TALES

The beginning of the school year was a different story, however. The beginning of every school year was torturous for Jake because he had to reveal himself to a new group of students. Every year Jake would be placed in a new classroom with some students who didn't know him, and he dreaded the moment when they realized he couldn't read. To Jake, every new classroom was filled with threats.

Table 4.2 Using UDL to Provide Options for Meeting the Common Core Writing Standards

Grade	Standard	Instructional Options
11/12	W.11-12.1.B Develop claim(s) and counterclaims fairly and thoroughly, supplying the most relevant evidence for each while pointing out strengths and limitations of both.	Students choose an article from one of the top-ten environmental blogs (http://bit.ly/1wNqUZT) or a popular political website (http://bit.ly/1BXiaDF) and respond to it on the blog, using evidence from the article and at least two other sources to make their claims and counter claims and presenting at least two perspectives on the topic. Students follow a Twitter strand of their choice and post four tweets on the topic, each succinctly portraying a different perspective on the topic.
9/10	L.9-10.3 Apply knowledge of language to understand how language functions in different contexts, to make effective choices for meaning or style and to comprehend more fully when reading or listening.	Students choose a topic relevant to their coursework or their personal interests and a point of view about that topic. They then have to write an opinion piece about that topic, including evidence, in three different formats. They can choose from formats such as a Facebook post, an informal e-mail to a friend, a formal e-mail to an editor, a blog post, an article for a newsletter, or a personal text. In each of the three formats, they must adjust the voice and style they use to be appropriate for the chosen format.
7	L7.3.A Choose language that expresses ideas precisely and concisely, recognizing and eliminating wordiness and redundancy.	Students choose a topic relevant to their coursework or their personal interests and write a thesis statement expressing an opinion about the topic. They then have to revise and clarify that thesis statement until it is short enough to tweet without eliminating any important information.
5	W.5.9.A Apply fifth-grade reading standards to literature(e.g., "Compare and contrast two or more characters, settings, or events in a story ora drama, drawing on specific details in the text.").	**Students choose one of the following options to compare characters from two pieces of literature.** Script and create a conversation between the characters using www.MakeBeliefsComix.com. The comic must clearly communicate the contrast between the characters. Create a Powtoon video that highlights the similarities and differences between the characters (www.powtoon.com).

Grade	Standard	Instructional Options
		Use www.voki.com to script and create two avatars, one for each character, clearly expressing the similarities and differences between them.
		Create a Venn diagram (either on computer or by hand on chart paper) that uses pictures, words, and phrases to compare the two characters.
3	W.3.7 Conduct short research projects that build knowledge about a topic.	**Students choose one of the following options to gather and organize information about a chosen topic.**
		Use www.Pinterest.com to create a board with pictures and information about their topic
		Create a slide show about their topic on iMovie, PowerPoint, Animotom, or Keynote.
		Create and organize a series of Post-it notes describing the information on their topic, either using real Post-it notes or virtual ones (www.padlet .com).
1	L.1.5.D Distinguish shades of meaning among verbs differing in manner (e.g. look, peek, glance, stare, glare, scowl) and adjectives differing in intensity (e.g. large, gigantic) by defining them or by acting out the meanings.	**Students choose one of the following options to illustrate the shades of meaning between a set of related verbs.**
		Use the camera on an iPad to take pictures of themselves acting out the meanings.
		Write sentences for each of the verbs (using either paper and pencil or technology) illustrating the differences in meaning.
		Create a time line showing the various verbs in order of intensity, either on paper or online (www.dipity .com).

At first, no one was aware of the struggle that occurred with Jake every August. He would come to his classes and sit quietly, never causing problems, trying hard to stay "under the radar," where no one would discover his learning problems. However, I soon noticed that Jake was not showing up for his reading intervention class in the afternoons. When I did a little investigation, I discovered that every day for the first two weeks of school, Jake had gone home sick at around ten o'clock. With a little more digging I found out that Jake, in order to avoid revealing himself to his new classmates, was going outside at recess in the hot August weather and running around as hard as he could until he was

completely overheated. Then he would go to the nurse's office and com-
plain that he wasn't feeling well. When the nurse took his temperature
he had a low-grade fever, and the nurse would call his mom to pick him
up. Clever Jake had figured out a way to avoid the threat inherent in his
new classroom. It was a brilliant and effective strategy!

When seeking to understand the concept of threat in the classroom, sometimes it's helpful to think of the opposite—how can we make our classes as safe and comfortable as possible for all learners? Additionally, if you think back to Chapter 1, "The Big Deal About Writing," you will remember that the cognitive and physical demands embedded in writing are inherently threatening to a large number of students. Our job, then, becomes to figure out ways to help our students feel supported and safe as they write.

Obviously, the first step is to create a classroom climate that accepts differences as normal. This is one of the places that UDL can truly be an asset. By providing *all* students with options about their work, we are taking away the stigma generally attached to differentiation. I would venture to say that, in most classes today, students with special learning needs are given accommodations that are different than what most of the other students are doing. Although this kind of differentiation can make the learning more accessible to those students, it also makes them stand out in the classroom. They are labeled as different by virtue of the different work they are doing.

In the UDL classroom, *every* student is given a variety of learning options. It's not just the student with dyslexia who is allowed to dictate an essay; every student is given that option. The culture we're creating when we set up our classrooms in this manner is one of engagement and acceptance. We are sending the message that every child has unique strengths and challenges and that all of them are accepted.

Ultimately, I promise you, those students who have the ability to use a pencil and paper to write essays will get enough practice doing so. Those students who have a true gift for writing will discover it and will explore and develop it through the wide variety of options you are giving them in the classroom. Students won't choose accommodations they don't need, but making them available to all removes stigma and any conversation of what is and isn't fair. Equally important, the students who have traditionally struggled with writing will feel empowered and motivated to do their very best work at their own level, with all the tools and strategies you've provided for them. They won't feel threatened to "reveal their weaknesses" because the classroom is set up to give everyone the same options. Just like the curb cut and the automatic door openers, the supports you've put in place for your struggling writers will be assets to every student in the class. If Jake had been a student in UDL classes, he wouldn't have felt the need to go home sick every day!

WRAPPING UP THE BIG IDEAS

- Engagement affects everything we do in the classroom and has a strong impact on the other principles of UDL.
- A culture of engagement empowers students and provides them with an understanding of their own learning strengths and the options to use them.
- Students need to learn about the hidden curriculum in writing in order to function successfully in the classroom.
- Teaching students to use technology so they can write independently will help them avoid learned helplessness, a common problem with struggling writers.
- Mastery-oriented feedback helps students focus on their growth and supports the development of metacognition.
- A balance of routine and novelty work is important, but some students may need to have choices that allow them to choose one over the other when they need to.
- By creating a culture that accepts and welcomes differences, we reduce the threats to those students whose learning patterns may stigmatize them in non-UDL classrooms.

Representation (Part One) 5

We can't just tell it; we have to show it.
We can't just show it; we have to define it.
We can't just define it; we have to manipulate it.
We can't just teach one way.

The National Center on Universal Design for Learning puts it this way: "To reduce barriers to learning, it is important to ensure that key information is equally perceptible to all learners by providing the same information through different modalities" (CAST, 2014). In other words, we need to not just *say* new information, we need to *show* it. We also need to use a *variety of methods* to show it so that learners have the opportunity to access the new information through the learning pathways that are most effective for each individual. Additionally, we need to give students the opportunity to manipulate and work with new information in a variety of ways. The good old days of "stand in front and lecture" are long gone! (And good riddance I say!) Think for a moment about the question below.

How do YOU most like to learn new information?

 By reading a great book

 By listening to a riveting storyteller

 By looking at beautiful visuals

 By experiencing a hands-on activity

I often give presentations to groups of teachers, parents, and administrators about UDL, and when I ask that question the group will usually be radically divided. There is likely to be at least one or two people for each preference, and there is often a majority who choose the last option—hands-on interactions with the topic. The moral, of course, is that we don't all learn the same way. That leads us to a story about Sammy and Sydni, two of my former students.

TEACHER'S TALES

Sammy and Sydni are brother and sister, and they were both students identified with learning disabilities who received services through my resource program. Despite having the same eligibility for special education, their learning profiles were completely different. Sammy, the younger of the siblings, had strong listening comprehension, and grasped new concepts easily. However, he had terrible difficulty learning to decode words, and his memory was poor; in fourth grade, Sammy was decoding at about a first-grade level. Sammy was what reading disability researchers would call dyslexic: he had poor phonemic skills and had trouble connecting sounds to symbols. Sydni, on the other hand, had the opposite profile. She was a good decoder who could read grade-level materials aloud with relative ease. However, Sydni's reading comprehension was poor, and she had difficulty understanding new concepts in all subject areas. Her overall language and vocabulary skills were low. Researchers might label Sydni as hyperlexic, a lesser-known term sometimes used to describe students who have strong decoding skills but weaknesses related to comprehension. Sammy and Sydni, despite being siblings and having the same special education eligibility (specific learning disability), learned best through completely different modalities. Sammy did well in a class where he could listen and absorb, while Sydni needed much more explicit, individualized interactions in most subject areas. Sammy needed remediation in phonics and fluency, while Sydni needed strategy instruction to help her read and comprehend.

The truth is that we have Sammys and Sydnis in all our classrooms, and UDL recognizes this as a natural diversity in our student populations. That's why a main principle of UDL is to provide *multiple options* for representation; in other words, we need to present new information in a variety of ways in order to make it easy for both our Sammys *and* our Sydnis (and all our other learners) to master it.

In a recent keynote address at an education conference, Margo Mastropieri and Tom Scruggs, two of the pioneers in learning strategies for students with learning disabilities, discussed some of the ongoing research in inclusive education. Their evidence from years of investigative studies shows the following: ***students with disabilities, when given the right kinds of supports, can learn general education content at proficient levels*** (Mastropieri & Scruggs, 2014). This means that given the right kind of intensive instruction, with the appropriate amount of scaffolding, opportunities for practice, and at an appropriate pace, students can master the curriculum. What do these supports look like in the area of writing? Well, their studies, plus those of other trailblazing researchers, such as Graham and Harris (mentioned in Chapter 1) and many others listed in the reference section at the end of the book have shown that students with disabilities benefit from several specific instructional techniques to become proficient writers:

1. **Explicitly teach the steps of the writing process**, using organizing strategies and tools that provide students with a plan to support and prompt them through the process.

2. **Explicitly teach, model, and dissect the different types of writing** they are expected to master.

3. **Provide many opportunities for recursive, guided feedback** with a teacher or a peer (Graham & Harris, 2013; Harris & Graham, 2013).

These three techniques meld nicely with the recommendations related to UDL representation, and we will discuss each of them in more detail within the CAST framework. But first, let's examine the three UDL guidelines for representation.

UDL Guideline #4: Options for Comprehension

Of course, as teachers we have to make our curriculum accessible for our learners, but once we've created accessibility, then the real work begins! We have to provide our learners with tools and strategies that will help them *go beyond access to understanding*. Students need to learn how to interpret, synthesize, transform, and apply new information, and this guideline helps teachers support those high-level skills. This guideline has a strong focus on the development of higher-order thinking, and is closely aligned to the demands of the CCSS. It also is particularly relevant to teachers who are working to create proficient writers. We will look at this guideline in detail in this chapter.

UDL Guideline #5: Options for
Language, Mathematical Expressions, and Symbols

As I discussed in the first chapter, many students with specific learning needs have weaknesses related to language, and in fact, all individuals vary in their ability to interpret linguistic and nonlinguistic information. Guideline #5 asks teachers to be aware of this variation and to provide support related to vocabulary, language conventions such as syntax, and symbols such as those found in graphs and charts. We will delve into this guideline, as well as #6, in Chapter 6.

UDL Guideline #6: Options for Perception

Guideline #6 is designed to ensure that teachers provide information through formats that are accessible to a wide variety of learners. For example, deaf students will need information provided in visual formats, while students with visual impairments will need auditory information; students with learning disabilities might benefit from either modality. It is this guideline that spurred us to create our learning options that you read about in the previous chapter. Don't forget you can return to them now at http://resources.corwin.com/spencerudl to look at the big ideas of this chapter in alternative formats.

GUIDELINE #4: SUPPORTING COMPREHENSION

Without a doubt, writing requires a lot of high-level thinking on the part of the student, and UDL Guideline #4 is focused on these higher-level skills—understanding, organizing, categorizing, and integrating information—all of which are inherent to the tasks of writing required by the Common Core writing standards. In addition to working on the *skills* embedded in writing, such as choosing vocabulary and managing syntax (which is covered in Chapter 6), students must generate ideas, organize them, and decide what and how to elaborate on them to create meaningful text. This is a challenging task for any writer but is particularly difficult for young people, who may not have strong capabilities in attending to a task, monitoring their work, and persisting long enough to revise and edit. These proficiencies, which involve both metacognition and executive functioning, will be examined in this UDL guideline.

Support Planning and Organization

When teaching students to write, one of the tried and true ways to help students plan and organize their writing is through the use of

graphic organizers. Graphic organizers can help clarify students' understanding of the structure of effective writing, and provide visual support
for students who have trouble processing information through auditory
channels.

I know that graphic organizers are not a new idea to teachers;
in fact, I'm sure that you are using graphic organizers already when
you teach writing. For some students, however, *how* you use those organizers may need to be adjusted. For example, you might teach the use
of one graphic organizer to help students brainstorm and organize their
ideas, another to organize their writing into paragraphs, a different
one to understand the grammatical and syntactical components of writing, and yet another to help students understand and master the writing
process.

Right now, I can hear my friend and colleague Dr. Kathy Rowlands,
who has done extensive work with secondary writing teachers through
the National Writing Project (www.nwp.org), whispering emphatically
in my ear, "Sally! Don't forget to mention that there isn't one graphic
organizer that will work for organizing all kinds of essays! If we only
teach students to use a five-paragraph organizer, as so many elementary schools do, they will struggle when they get to high school and they
need to write something that doesn't fit into that structure." As Kathy
reminds us, we also need to teach students to be flexible in their planning. Teaching students a variety of writing organizers for the tasks at
hand, and how to choose thoughtfully between them, is a critical element for proficiency.

In addition to using a variety of organizers throughout the writing
process and learning to be flexible with their use, we also have to scaffold
our teaching to help our students learn to use the organizers independently and even to create their own organizers to use on assessments.
One of my proudest teaching moments came when the mom of one of
my fifth graders, Caitlin, came to me about two years after she had left
elementary school to tell me that Caitlin was still using the graphic organizing strategy that I had taught her and that it was helping her succeed
on her middle school essays. If you can teach a student to value and
use a strategy on her own, then you have truly taught her a skill that
can change her life. Scaffolding the teaching and gradually withdrawing
support are two of the strategies critical to helping struggling learners
become proficient writers.

Some students have an easy time organizing themselves as they
prepare to write. Facts, information, vocabulary, and other necessary
elements come effortlessly to them, and many can even pull up the

knowledge they need on the spot as they write. For others, however, this is not such a simple task. Think back to Chapter 1 and the story of Brian—fifth grader Brian was so overwhelmed by the cognitive demands inherent in writing that he temporarily forgot how to write the letter K. For Brian (and many other students), it is critically important to "get his ducks in a row" before he writes by activating and organizing his knowledge. For these students, the explicit teaching of organizing strategies is imperative.

*Researchers Russell Gersten and Scott Baker did a meta-analysis of writing studies conducted over about fifteen years, and discovered that one of the elements that consistently helped students with disabilities improve their writing was what they called a **procedural facilitator**. A procedural facilitator was any tool designed to help students understand the processes needed to successfully complete a piece of writing (Gersten & Baker, 2001). A procedural facilitator could be a mnemonic device, such as an acronym that provides a set of steps to follow, a graphic organizer, or a combination of both. What is important is not so much the tool you use as how you use it. For struggling learners to be successful, they must be allowed to use the same facilitator (or tool) until they are comfortable with it, can implement it on their own, and are able use it to guide their conversation about the process of writing.*

In fact, the folks at Vanderbilt University's Project Write (2009), the creators of many highly researched and validated writing strategies, say this on their website: **"The power is not in the mnemonic, but in how well the mnemonic represents the genre, and how the mnemonic is taught."** In other words, as the teacher, your job is not to find the one "magic" organizer that will solve all your students' problems but to teach them a variety of tools that will work in different contexts, genres, and for different purposes and then to teach the use of those tools explicitly, to mastery. Once the students know how to use the tools independently, you can begin to help them learn how to choose the best tool for different writing applications.

The process for teaching these types of learning strategies has been heavily researched and validated with populations of struggling learners, and no matter what mnemonic strategy or graphic organizer you use, the experts recommend you follow the steps in Table 5.1 to teach it. These steps should be spread out over a series of days or even weeks, and students will need plenty of opportunities to internalize and practice as they

Table 5.1   Steps for Teaching a Learning Strategy

How to Explicitly Teach a Graphic Organizer or Mnemonic Strategy	
1. Develop Background Knowledge	In this step, you need to assess and teach the vocabulary and concepts a student will need to know in order to learn your mnemonic or organizer. For example, if you are teaching a paragraph strategy and your student doesn't really understand the concept of a topic sentence, you would need to teach that concept first. The key here is to identify the prerequisite skills and concepts a student needs for your strategy and to preteach them in step one.
2. Discuss the Strategy	Here your job is to motivate your learners to use the strategy and help them begin to understand when and why to use it. The research is clear—struggling learners will not apply strategies unless someone explicitly explains to them how they will help. That's our job in step two!
3. Model It	In this step, you explicitly teach the strategy by demonstrating how it is used. The most effective way to do this is often through a think-aloud; step into the role of the learner and talk yourself through the steps of the strategy, verbalizing your thought processes and questions along the way. This step is critically important to the success of any strategy instruction, and it may have to be done more than once before all your students will master it. Small group instruction can be really helpful for students who need a little more practice.
4. Memorize It	By now most of your students should have some understanding of how to use the strategy, so it's important that they begin to use it on their own. Before they can do that, however, they will need to know the steps by heart. This doesn't mean they have to memorize the strategy word for word, but it does mean that they need to be able to generate the steps *in order from memory* and explain what they mean. Giving students the opportunity to memorize the steps through activities such as flash cards, rehearsal, and the use of picture cues will help them commit the steps to memory so they can move on to the next step, practice.
5. Support It	At this point, your students are ready to practice with the strategy. Like any other skill you teach them, they need various levels of practice in order to prepare them to work independently. Providing them the opportunity to practice in groups, with partners, and with frequent peer and teacher feedback will lead them down the road to mastery and help them to use the strategy independently.
6. Establish Independent Practice	Hooray! Our students have begun to internalize the steps of the strategy, and they are ready to use it on their own. But don't stop supporting them yet—monitor their use of the strategy, and make sure they are using the steps appropriately. Although small changes may be okay, you want to keep an eye on their progress to make sure they haven't meaningfully altered the strategy so that it becomes ineffective. And give yourself a pat on the back for having explicitly taught that strategy to mastery!

Source: Harris and Graham (1996).

go along. *You may be tempted to jump right to step three,* but I urge you not to. The first two steps have been shown to be incredibly important to students with learning challenges and are the pieces that can make the difference between the strategy being a success or a failure.

Remember, these steps will help your students learn to independently use a graphic organizer too. Many teachers assume that once a student has seen a teacher model the use of a graphic organizer, he will know how to use it, but research tells us that isn't so. Lots of students need explicit teaching like the Self-Regulated Strategy Development (SRSD) in order to make use of learning strategies such as mnemonics and graphic organizers. If you make these steps part of your teaching repertoire, soon you will see many more of your students mastering the tools you provide for them. Trust me—over time the process will begin to seem natural, you will be able to move through the steps relatively quickly, and as you see your students master the tools, the SRSD will no longer seem like a bothersome add-on to your teaching load.

The POW+TREE Model. One of the most extensively researched tools for students who struggle with writing is the POW+TREE mnemonic device. It is actually two tools in one—POW stands for **p**ick an idea or topic, **o**rganize and generate ideas, and **w**rite and say more. TREE stands for the parts of each paragraph: **t**opic sentence, **r**easons, **e**xplanation, and **e**nding. The two interact in an overlapping manner, so it looks like the example in Table 5.2.

For more information on the use of SRSD to teach learning strategies and the POW+TREE model, explore the modules developed by Vanderbilt University's IRIS Center. These modules contain a wealth of information about teaching students with disabilities and are in a format that is accessible and very teacher-friendly. The module on SRSD can be found at http://iris.peabody.vanderbilt.edu/module/srs/#content. There are also many POW+TREE teaching materials available on the Vanderbilt website at http://kc.vanderbilt.edu/projectwrite.

There are many different tools that you, as a teacher, can use to help your students activate and organize their background knowledge before writing. The strategy you choose to employ will most likely be determined by the type of writing your students are doing. Since the CCSS divide writing into three different types, it makes sense that you might need different types of organizers for each type of writing. In practice, however, expository writing, such as argument and information, lends itself to one type of organizer, and the more linear nature of narrative writing correlates with different types of organizing tools. We will look at a few below.

Table 5.2 The POW+TREE Mnemonic Strategy

Pick an idea/topic and state it clearly.	Formulate your topic or opinion.
Organize your ideas and generate more.	Complete a graphic organizer or other organizing tool.
Topic sentence	Formulate a topic sentence that clearly states the main idea.
Reason	Generate reasons to support your main idea.
Explanation	Clearly explain your reasons.
Ending	Summarize your paragraph with a clear statement.
write and say more!	Expand on what you've written.

Source: Project Write (2009).

In general, simple graphic organizers are better. If our goal is to help students generalize the learning of the graphic organizers to the point where they can use them on their own and recreate them when they aren't there, choosing simpler organizers and teaching them to mastery will be your best strategy!

INSIDER TIPS

Organizers for Expository Writing. Both argument and informational writing require students to cluster ideas around topics and expand on them within that framework. However, there are some critical differences in terms of how the ideas should be organized. Figures 5.1 and 5.2 show two graphic organizers for first grade, one for an opinion piece and one for informational writing. As you can see, the two organizers have some commonalities that should make it easier for a student to apply what they learn about one organizer to the other one. This is the key to teaching *flexible* use of graphic organizers to students. Use the explicit teaching of the SRSD to teach and master one type of organizer, then help students transfer that learning to another type that more closely fits the demands of a different genre or style of writing. Figures 5.3 and 5.4 show a similar relationship between organizers designed for the fourth-grade standards. Again, students should be able to learn and practice one of the organizers and then easily transfer that understanding to the other.

As students get older, the demands and the organization get more complex, but the concept still remains—teach them to use one organizer until they can use it independently, and then help them generalize and apply it to another structure. Figures 5.5 and 5.6 show examples at the ninth- or tenth-grade level. As you look at all six of the organizers, you should also be able to see how the same organizational concepts develop through the grade levels, just as they do in the CCSS. Schools and districts who use a consistent set of tools across grade levels will find their students much more able to use them independently and generalize the learning to new tools (Santangelo, Harris, & Graham, 2008).

Pay attention to this idea of adapting the organizers. We want to teach our students the principles behind using a graphic organizer, and then help them learn how to tweak them to suit the needs of a particular piece of writing. So, for example, you might teach a secondary student to use the organizer in Figure 5.5, then have her expand that use by generating two reasons for each claim and counter-claim. It is the same principle but now applied to a more complex piece of writing. A struggling fourth grader might use the organizer in Figure 5.3 to generate only one opinion with two details and then gradually move up to two, three, or even four as his proficiency grows.

When choosing organizers for planning, it's important that you choose those that do not encourage students to "jump in and start writing." Your goal is for students to activate their prior knowledge and organize the information, not to begin writing complete sentences. For most students, a Cloze-format organizer would not be effective in this stage of writing. (For example, you might find an organizer that looks something like this: "I think _____. My reasons are _____.") This type of organizer encourages students to skip the organizing step and go straight to writing sentences, a practice which will be ineffective over the long run for most struggling writers.

I know I've said it before, but I need to reiterate this important point: **the specific type of organizer you use is not as important as how you use it**. Teaching students the parts of the organizer, modeling its use over multiple applications, and supporting the students as they begin to use it on their own will create writers who know how to plan their writing in a variety of types of writing. And here's one more significant detail to consider: good writers know how to *talk* about their writing.

First Grade W.1.1: Write opinion pieces in which they introduce the topic or name the book they are writing about, state an opinion, supply a reason for the opinion, and provide some sense of closure.

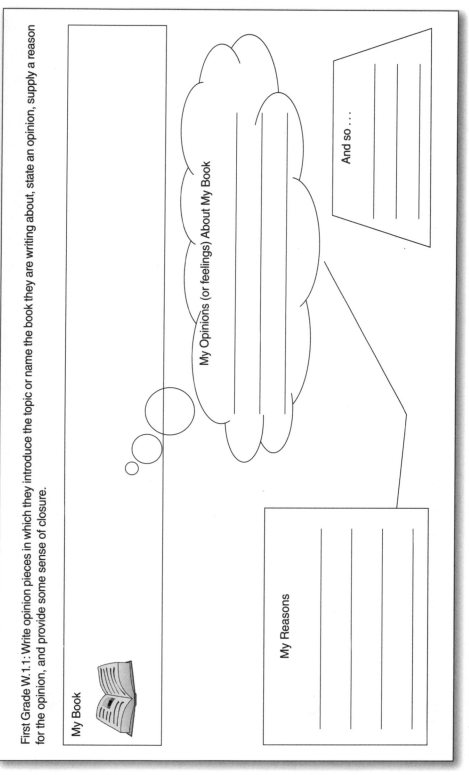

My Book

My Opinions (or feelings) About My Book

And so . . .

My Reasons

Figure 5.2 Graphic Organizer for Activating and Organizing Prior Knowledge to Write an Informational Piece in Primary Grades (W.1)

Second Grade W.1.2: Write informative/explanatory texts in which they name a topic, supply some facts about the topic, and provide some sense of closure.

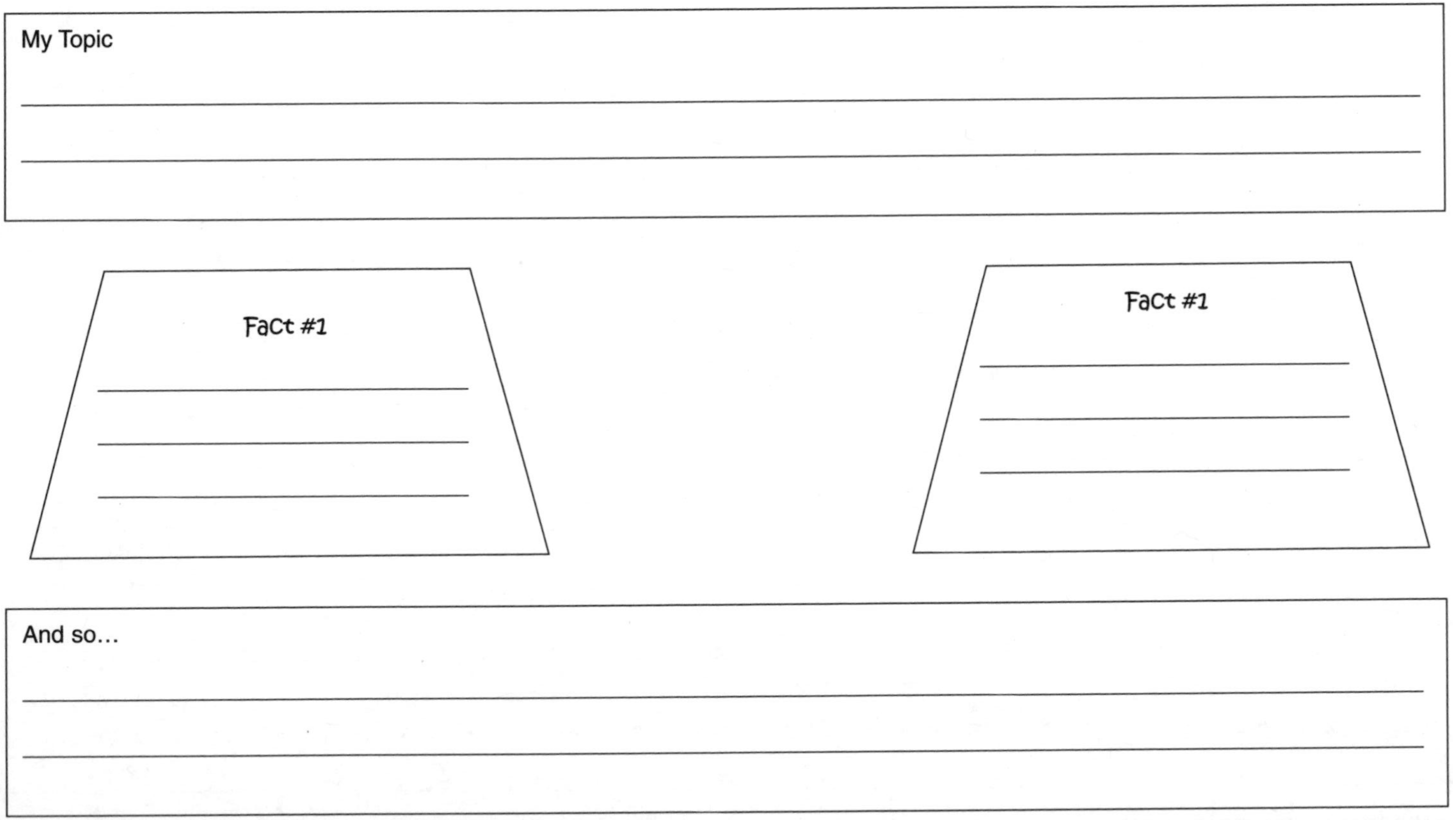
My Topic
Fact #1
Fact #1
And so…

Fourth Grade W.4.1.A: Introduce a topic or text clearly, state an opinion, and create an organizational structure in which related ideas are grouped to support the writer's purpose. W.4.1.B: Provide reasons that are supported by facts and details.

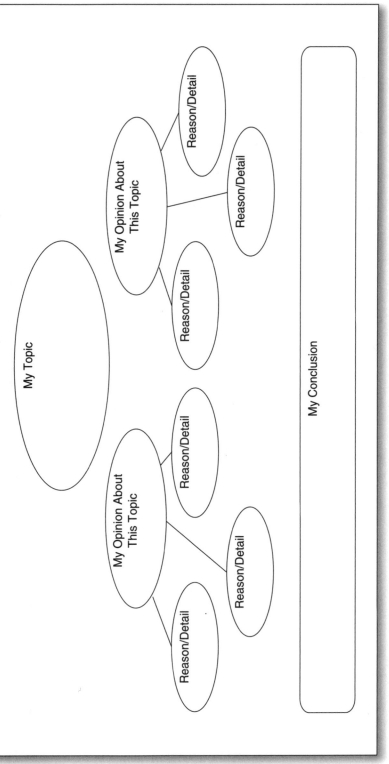

Figure 5.4 Graphic Organizer for Activating and Organizing Prior Knowledge for an Informative or Factual Essay, Primary Grades (W.2)

Fourth Grade W.4.2.A: Introduce a topic clearly and group related information in paragraphs and sections. W.4.2.B: Develop the topic with facts, definitions, concrete details.

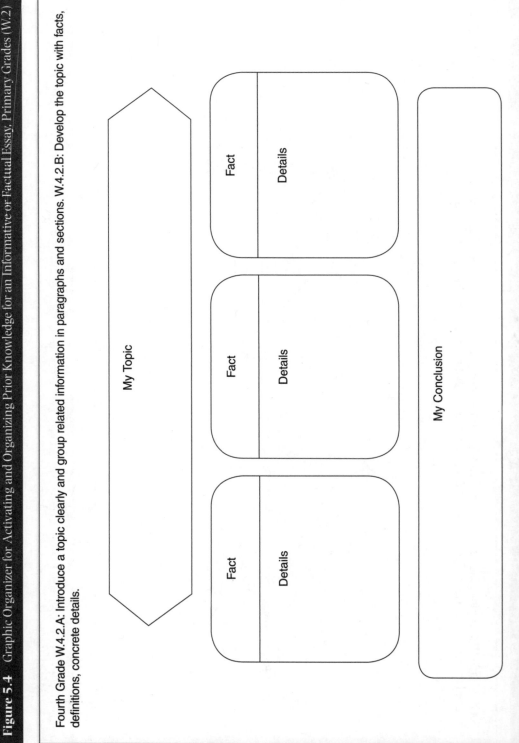

My Topic

Fact

Details

Fact

Details

Fact

Details

My Conclusion

Ninth/Tenth Grade W.9–10.1: Write arguments to support claims in an analysis of substantive topics or texts, using valid reasoning and relevant and sufficient evidence.

Claim	Counter-Claim
Reason	Reason
Evidence	Evidence
Evidence	Evidence
My Conclusion	

Figure 5.6 Graphic Organizer for Activating and Organizing Prior Knowledge for an Informative or Factual Essay. Middle Grades (W.2)

Ninth/Tenth Grade W.9–10.2.A: Introduce a topic; organize ideas, concepts, and information. W.9–10.2.B: Develop the topic with well-chosen, relevant and sufficient facts, extended definitions, concrete details, quotations, and other information and examples.

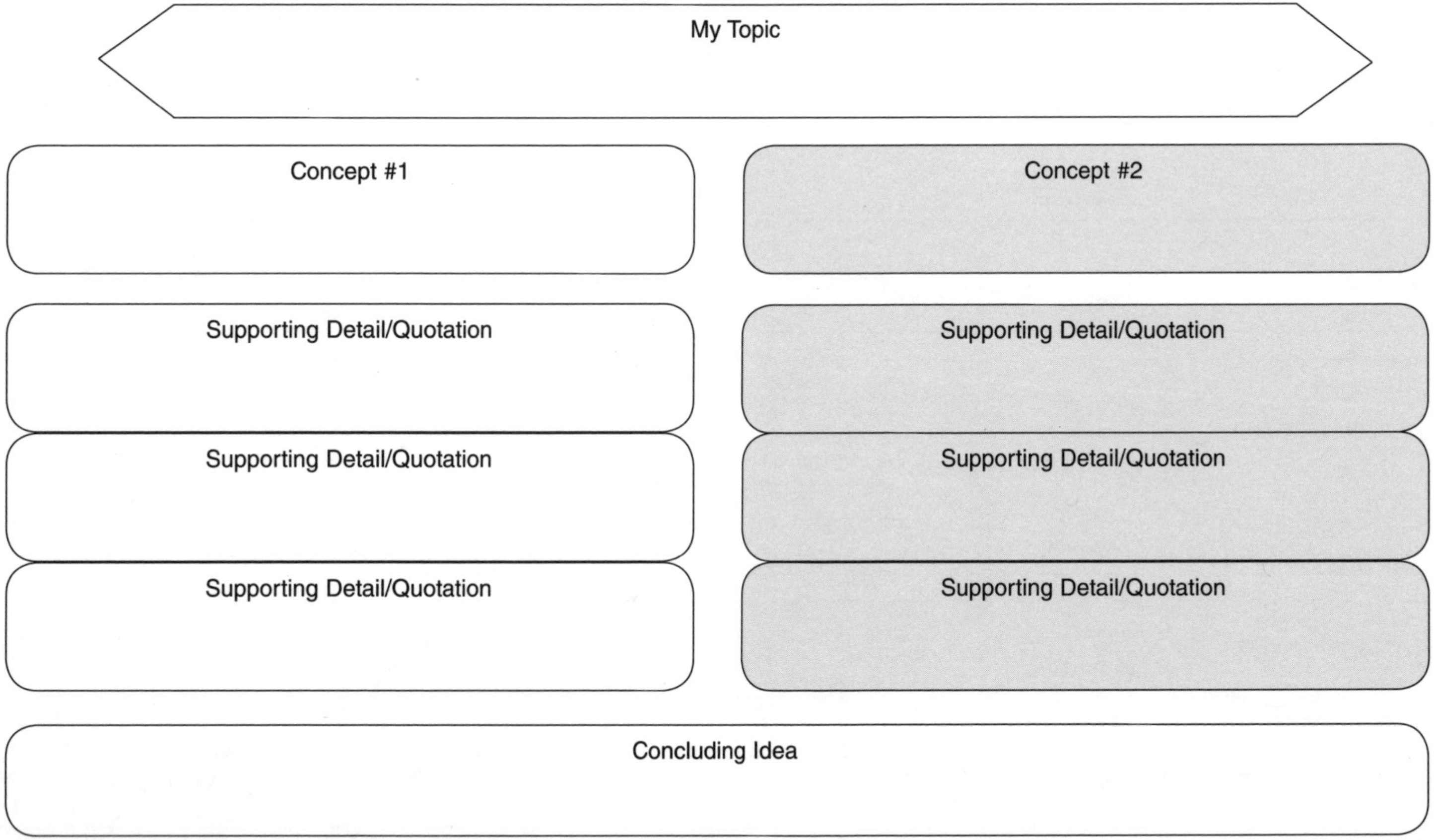

My Topic

Concept #1	Concept #2
Supporting Detail/Quotation	Supporting Detail/Quotation
Supporting Detail/Quotation	Supporting Detail/Quotation
Supporting Detail/Quotation	Supporting Detail/Quotation

Concluding Idea

Use your graphic organizers as a means to help students develop language about writing. Encourage class and small group discussions around the elements in the organizers, and insist that students use the language in the organizers when they ask you questions or request assistance. It's important to use the tools to develop concepts, not just as a notepad for writing down ideas.

Teaching and using graphic organizers like this will help students understand that an important first step in writing is to plan. Making the organizers consistent yet flexible and adapting them to the specific demands of each writing task will help students appreciate that even though there are different types of writing assignments and the demands for completing them may vary, the same basic processes still apply: you need to gather and organize your thoughts before you write. In fifth grade, you might have students plan a five-paragraph essay, then a three-paragraph essay, then a seven- or eight-paragraph essay (or one paragraph, if that's what your students need), and use the same organizer each time, adapting to the new demands.

Many educators have done wonderful work creating organizers that help students learn to plan their writing. Table 5.3 (p. 82) includes links to a variety of tools that you may choose to use in your classroom. Some are free; others require you to subscribe to a website or buy a book. Some of these tools are available only as paper copies, others can be accessed and completed on the Web, which is of course a wonderful way to provide options for your students who prefer to work digitally. *All can be effective if used systematically with your students and if taught and modeled strategically, offering opportunities for students to practice and apply them to different types of writing.* I encourage you to explore and experiment and find the combination of organizers that is most effective for your students and for you as a skilled teacher of writing.

For students who need more significant supports, consider creating prompts, pictures, and choices within the organizers. See Figure 5.7 (p. 83), which is a more-supported version of Figure 5.4. The student chose the topic of reptiles, so the teacher provided word and picture prompts to help him organize his writing. A Cloze sentence is used to help the student begin to generate an opinion or feeling to end the piece, although this may be modified in a later draft.

Graphic organizers for narrative writing. The graphic organizers we've presented so far help students to identify and organize the big ideas in expository style writing (W.1 and W.2). However, in narrative writing (W.3), it is not unusual to see students begin to write a story

Table 5.3 Tools for Planning

Tool	What It Is	Available At
Differentiated Visual Tools	Interactive graphic organizer software for struggling writers featuring discipline-specific visuals individually designed to target specific Common Core Standards. Software is purchased, but free samples are available.	http://www .MakesSenseStrategies.com Soon to be available as online interactive components
Literacy TA	A website with oodles of teacher materials, most aligned to the CCSS. Lots of writing organizers and lesson plans. $50 yearly membership or one-week free trial.	http://www.literacyta.com
ReadWriteThink	The website of the International Reading Association, with dozens of free teacher resources, including many graphic organizers and some online interactive graphic organizers.	http://www.readwritethink .org http://www.readwritethink .org/classroom-resources/ student-interactives/story -30008.html
Kidspiration	Online tool for creating graphic organizers, with tools specifically geared toward students in Grades K–5. Pictures and webs can be converted to outline format with the click of a button. iPad version available.	http://www.inspiration.com/ Kidspiration
Inspiration	The adult version of Kidspiration is designed to be used by students in Grades 6 and up. Again, diagrams and mind maps can be converted to outline format.	http://www.inspiration.com
Bubbl.us	An online brainstorming tool for creating and sharing graphic organizers. The free version allows up to three organizers, and for a fee, you can get unlimited organizers and can include pictures and graphics.	https://bubbl.us

Figure 5.7 Graphic Organizer for Activating and Organizing Prior Knowledge for an Informative or Factual Essay, Primary Grades (W.2)

Fourth Grade W.4.2.A: Introduce a topic clearly and group related information in paragraphs and sections. W.4.2.B: Develop the topic with facts, definitions, concrete details.

For students who need more support:

My Topic

Reptiles

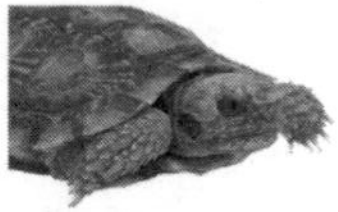

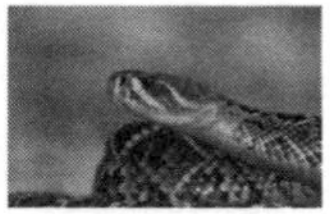

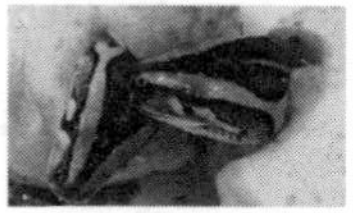

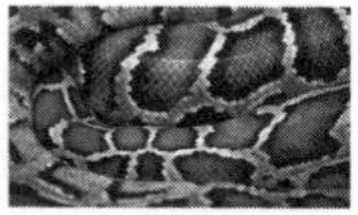

Two Types of Reptiles

____

____

Two Facts About Reptiles

____

____

My Conclusion

I think reptiles are ______________ and ______________.

that trails off into an endless string of related but unorganized events joined by the words "then" and "next." Students need tools to help them generate and sort their ideas when they are writing narrative essays as well.

When teaching narrative writing, there are some engaging ways we can help students organize their ideas before they begin to write. One of the most popular is storyboarding. Storyboards are a wonderful tool to help the students focus on the big ideas of a story before they begin writing. When they are creating storyboards, we want them to use as few words as possible to describe the sequence of events. As with most tools, we need to model and explicitly teach storyboarding, or students may quickly fall into bad habits, trying to jump in and write full pieces of the storyline while making their storyboard or cartoon. Take a look at the two examples in Figures 5.8 and 5.9.

The first example, which was created using the free version of www.StoryboardThat.com, shows a student who has run amok using the storyboard tool. Since our goal for using storyboards is to generate and organize big ideas, not to write a graphic novel, we want to discourage students from writing a lot of text. Even though this example seems sophisticated, in fact, it took more than an hour to create, and it only covers the very beginning of the story. The second example is a more appropriate use of storyboarding to organize the big ideas of a narrative story. The second one was created using www.bitstrips.com, a free app for tablets and phones. (It's important to note that both tools are great for storyboarding. It's the application of the tool that makes it effective!)

One of the advantages to using an online tool like this is that the tool itself stimulates students' imaginations. Just as UDL suggests, those who may have trouble thinking of something to write can benefit from the opportunity to brainstorm using tools and apps such as these. The wide variety of characters and settings that come in the programs help students come up with creative ideas that they might not otherwise have considered.

There are other great digital storyboarding tools and programs that can help students plan their narrative essays, some of which I've listed in Table 5.4. Some will work for informational essays as well. If you don't have access to technology, a simple storyboard template can be downloaded for free from www.printablepaper.net/category/storyboard or you can make your own. If you decide to go the paper route, however, don't leave too much room on the paper for writing; remember, your goal is to have them write just a few words for each picture to get at the big ideas. Students who don't like to draw can search images on the Internet or in magazines and paste them into the outline.

Figure 5.8 Inappropriate Use of Storyboarding With Too Much Text and Detail

Figure 5.9 More Appropriate Use of Storyboarding to Outline the Big Ideas of the Story

Table 5.4 Digital Tools for Creating Storyboards

Tool	What It Is	Available At
Storyboard That	Online storyboard site that gives you dozens of settings, characters, and shapes to help you create detailed cartoons. Can be a little awkward to use at first, but the free version has a pretty good selection of icons.	http://www.storyboardthat.com
Bitstrips	App for iPad or Android that allows you to make very detailed cartoons with a wide range of characters and settings. Very user-friendly and fun!	http://www.bitstrips.com
Creating Storyboards	Created by the University of Hawaii, this page walks you through the important steps of organizing and creating storyboards using a variety of digital tools.	http://digitalstorytelling.coe.uh.edu/page.cfm?id=23&cid=23&sublinkid=37

Another important planning strategy is to help students generate ideas about their characters, either characters from texts they've read or ones they are creating for their own original narrative writing. Hang a chart in your class of potential character traits appropriate to your grade level so that students can reference it when they are creating or describing characters, and be sure to teach the meanings of the traits explicitly, using a variety of visual examples. Readwritethink.org provides an extensive list of character traits at http://www.readwritethink.org/files/resources/lesson_images/lesson175/traits.pdf.

Figure 5.10 is another example from bitstrips.com. Here I used it to create a character and to flesh out some of his character traits. The background scenes, clothing, facial expressions, and other features of the app helped me come up with a character that almost created himself. Who knew "Simon" would end up being a veterinarian? For students who have trouble generating ideas, they can use comic apps to create well-developed characters before they write. And when they are done, they have a concrete, visual representation of their characters that will no doubt help them write their narratives.

Figure 5.10 Using a Cartoon Program to Create a Character

Highlight Patterns and Relationships in Writing

As your students begin to learn about the different types of writing covered under the CCSS, they will need your help to process that information and make meaning of it. Some students will do that naturally, but the majority of students will need specific instruction and guidance to begin to synthesize and apply their new learning. CAST recommends providing interactive models to students with gradual scaffolding of the new information. One of the most interesting and productive ways to do this is by spending time comparing and dissecting different types of writing. This is in perfect alignment with CC Writing Standard 10 (W.10), and more importantly, it can help your students identify and make sense of the patterns and skills embedded in writing that may apply to multiple genres.

Luckily for us, the folks at Common Core have provided sample papers that can be used as a starting place to discuss the three main types of writing covered by the CCSS—you can find them in Common Core Appendix C. I recommend giving students the opportunity to delve deeply into these sample papers as well as others (see Table 5.5 for sources) and then dig into other types of writing such as e-mails, poetry, blogs, and social media, discussing and comparing what these types of writing have in common and what is different. Do they all require the same type of planning? If not, what is different? Do they all need to be edited and revised, and if so, is that process the same? Do some kinds of writing require more of one thing than another? Why or why not? How do they compare in terms of the time it takes to write them? Do they all have distinctive beginning and endings? How are the endings the same and how are they different? These questions and more can be used to gradually uncover the commonalities and distinctions in different styles of writing.

For this type of instruction to be effective with struggling learners, the conversations should begin at a young age. In second grade, the discussion might sound something like this:

Teacher:	Does this passage have a good beginning?
Student 1:	Yes!
Teacher:	Why? What's good about it?
Student 1:	It tells what it is about.
Teacher:	It does! Can anyone think of another way we could start this story?
Student 2:	I got a computer for Christmas.
Student 3:	He likes his computer.
Student 4:	I like to play with my new computer every day.
Teacher (writing down the suggestions):	Thank you! Let's discuss these and see which we like the best.

This type of instruction works really well in small groups, where every student will have the maximum opportunity to participate. For struggling writers you need to have this type of conversation consistently, with lots of opportunities to apply the thinking to new samples and with maximum feedback from the teacher and peers. For optimum effectiveness, teams of teachers should discuss using common language and common practice structures across grade levels.

I encourage you to provide both strong and weak models of different types of writing to compare and discuss. One of the drawbacks of the samples provided by the CCSS is that they are mostly very strong examples at each grade level. While it's important for students to see high-quality samples to which they can aspire, equally important, I believe, is discussing ways to improve weaker samples. This is the process that your struggling writers will need to complete with their own work, and spending time critiquing and improving essays (particularly in small groups) can significantly improve students' abilities to edit their own work. Table 5.5 gives you resources for sample papers across the grade levels, many of which are annotated to help you identify salient points. I also recommend collecting work samples from your students, taking the names off of them, and using them with your next year's class. Authentic work samples that reflect your student population and culture can be the best tools of all.

Maximizing Generalization

The in-depth analysis of writing samples we've discussed above will also help students take what they learn about one type of writing and generalize it to others. Comparing the planning of an e-mail, for example, to an informational essay will help students understand that even an e-mail needs some mental organization. The teacher's job becomes to help students take the system they've learned for one type of writing, such as the graphic organizer presented in Figure 5.4, and apply it to another type of writing, such as writing a blog. Do we still need a main idea? What would that look like in a blog? Do we still want to present three facts? If not, what will the content be instead? Will a personal blog be the same as a professional blog? What kind of conclusion do we need?

Table 5.5 Sources for Writing Samples

Source	What You'll Find
http://www.ttms.org/ PDFs/03%20Writing%20 Samples%20v001%20(Full).pdf	A variety of samples, Grades K–12, not annotated. These samples tend to be a little lower level than those provided by the CCSS, so they're useful for discussing improvements.
http://www.readingrockets .org/looking_at_writing	Beautifully annotated samples, Grades K–3.
http://achievethecore.org/ content/upload/ ArgumentOpinion_K-12WS.pdf	Annotated samples of argument/opinion essays, Grades K–12, with teacher script and discussion points.
http://achievethecore.org	The home page of the site above, this has links to hundreds of student writing samples, as well as lesson plans and assessments.

Whether you are teaching kindergarten or twelfth grade, your students, especially those who struggle to write effectively, need structured, teacher-guided opportunities to analyze and apply what they've learned to different purposes and genres. Without your guidance, only the most capable of writers will understand how to transfer what they've learned to new writing structures.

The same applies to the mnemonic devices we discussed earlier in this chapter. The POW-TREE mnemonic was designed to be used with expository writing, but the principles behind it can apply to many other types of writing. Help your students make that generalization by explicitly teaching how the parts of such a mnemonic can be helpful to students writing e-mails, for example. Do we still need to (**P**) pick an idea or topic? Sure! Even an e-mail or letter needs to have a purpose. Do we still need to (**O**) organize and generate our ideas? Yes, although that process may or may not be as explicit as it is for our essays, depending on the purpose of the e-mail. As with the graphic organizers, teaching students to take the structures and use them fluidly for different types of writing will help your students learn to write effectively across a variety of applications.

WRAPPING UP THE BIG IDEAS

- Different students learn in different ways, so we need to provide multiple ways for students to access new knowledge.
- Mnemonic devices and graphic organizers help struggling learners learn and make meaning of new ideas more successfully, but they have to be taught systematically and explicitly to mastery.
- Students with writing challenges need to be explicitly taught how to organize their writing by using graphic organizers that are adapted for different types of writing, and how to generalize that knowledge to new types of writing.
- Analyzing and comparing different types of writing, and writing for different purposes, will help students maximize transfer of the knowledge to new genres.
- To help students understand how to improve their own writing, it's important to analyze strong as well as weaker examples of student writing.

Representation (Part Two)   **6**

We can't just show it; we have to show it in a way that students can understand.
We can't just define it; we have to give multiple definitions in a variety of contexts.
We can't just teach one way.

GUIDELINE #5: SUPPORTING STUDENTS' UNDERSTANDING OF LANGUAGE

As we know, the heart of UDL lies in providing options. Since your classroom is likely to have students with all different levels of language ability, it is up to you as the teacher to present new information in a variety of ways so that it's accessible to all of them. Research has shown time and time again that teachers tend to teach the way they were taught. For most of us, that means an emphasis on teacher talk with minimal visual supports. Unfortunately, in today's diverse classrooms, that type of teaching will leave a lot of students behind. In this section, we are going to look at representation strategies that are tied into the Common Core language standards, beginning with ideas to clarify students' understanding of vocabulary (L.4, L.5, and L.6). Remember, the language standards are geared toward the *skills* of writing, including grammar, language conventions, and vocabulary.

Clarifying Vocabulary

Vocabulary knowledge has been identified as one of the key areas in which students with disabilities fall behind. That isn't terribly surprising since the majority of students with disabilities are struggling readers, and struggling readers read much less than their proficient counterparts. Because they read less, they are exposed to fewer new words (Stanovich, 1986), which makes it that much harder for them to produce grade-level appropriate writing. However, teaching vocabulary is tricky. Just because a student learns the word *preposterous* doesn't mean that she can generalize it to *outrageous* or *ridiculous*. Unfortunately, vocabulary doesn't work like that.

It's clear, then, that teaching and clarifying vocabulary is particularly important for students with learning challenges, hence its focus in UDL. In order to best make use of limited vocabulary time, CAST emphasizes the importance of helping students learn new words by *creating connections to previously known words* (CAST, 2014). One of the best ways to help students create cognitive connections to support new vocabulary is by teaching them Latin and Greek roots and the words that share them.

Latin and Greek Roots

Beginning in Grade 4, the Common Core language standards require that students gain knowledge of common Latin and Greek word roots and parts. This requirement continues in the standards through Grade 8 (L.4.4.B – L.8.4.B). Research tells us that learning common words parts is a very effective way to increase students' vocabulary knowledge because affixes and roots can apply to a large number of words and can provide clues to the meanings of new words. In fact, of English words with more than one syllable, approximately 90 percent of them have Latin roots, and a single Latin root can be linked to literally dozens of words (Rasinski, Padak, Newton, & Newton, 2008). Since the CCSS don't tell us specifically what roots to focus on at each grade level, it is left to the discretion of the teacher, school, or curriculum designer to make that decision.

The Internet provides us with some great tools to support this work. For example, www.wordinfo.info is a search engine that gives definitions of words related to a common root, with vocabulary cartoons and links to other words with related roots. It is a terrific resource for teachers. Similarly, www.onelook.com will search multiple dictionaries to create a word list from any word root, giving you an excellent starting point for choosing words to study. To use onelook.com, type the root in the search box with an asterisk in front and back. For example, if you wanted to look up the root "spect," you would type "spect," into the box. (The asterisks tell the search engine that you want to find all words that contain spect somewhere in the word.) When your search appears, filter the search by clicking on "Common Word," and voilà! You will have an extensive list of words that include your root. (In this case, the search identified seventy-three different words that include the root spect.) This unique search engine will also allow you to search by parts of speech, meaning, and a variety of other options. Click "wildcard" on the home page to see all of the search options available through onelook.com.

In their book *Greek & Latin Roots: Keys to Building Vocabulary* (2008), Timothy Rasinski and his colleagues recommend a daily vocabulary routine that includes breaking words down and putting them together, applying them in context, and providing lots of practice with related words through an assortment of game-like activities. This is a great example of UDL in action—teachers can provide options for understanding by giving students a variety of experiences with the target words every day. What's important here is the *variety of activities* that make the learning accessible to different types of learners. Students explore the word meanings through deep processing activities. They integrate new words with previously learned vocabulary to build schema. They break words down and compare them to other words to help them build connections and generalize the learning. And they get plenty of practice in a high-interest format. The authors present a diversity of motivating activities such as acting out the meanings of words, Wordo (an adaptation of Bingo), Root Word Riddles, and card games for practice.

I particularly like the game of Scattergories, one of the practice strategies the authors recommend to help students apply their knowledge of roots and affixes. In Scattergories for root words, students are provided with a matrix that has roots along one side and affixes along the other and are challenged to work in groups to generate as many words as they can using the specified elements (Table 6.1).

UDL also recommends displaying information graphically as well as in words. There are many different graphic organizers available to help students understand the concept of root words, prefixes, and suffixes, and, as we discussed in Chapter 5, the specific one you choose isn't as important as teaching one explicitly and using it consistently for a variety of words. The strategic application of a graphic organizer over time will help struggling learners internalize and generalize the learning, and after many chances to practice, most learners should be able to use the organizer independently. Here are a few of my favorites:

Table 6.1 Scattergories for Greek and Latin Roots

Roots	trans	re	tion/ation
form			
ject			
act			

Source: Rasinski et al. (2004).

Teacher Sara Wiley uses a graphic organizer of a bicycle to help students understand how the prefix and suffix go together. The full organizer can be downloaded from www.smekenseducation.com.

The idea of using a tree (with the root on the roots) has been utilized by many. It is a great way to create a useful word list from Latin and Greek roots. For older students, the same graphic strategy can apply, but use a more sophisticated depiction of a tree. The point of all these activities, of course, is to help students identify that there are word parts common to many words and that meaning can often be inferred through these word parts.

I love www.bubbl.us as a tool for creating all kinds of graphic organizers. In this case, I've used it to make a root word organizer that shows the relationships between words with the same root and points out the similarities between affixes. I used our word list from onelook.com as a resource to create this!

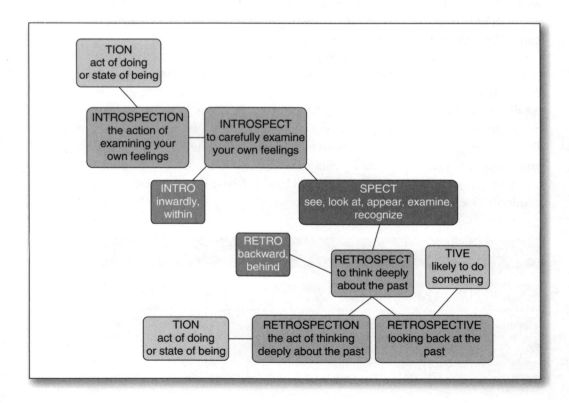

*Caitlyn was one of my all-time favorite students. She was bright, talented, and fun to work with. Caitlyn was in my resource program for several years and during that time became proficient with a variety of tools that we used in our classroom. One day, about nine months after Caitlyn graduated from elementary school, there was a knock on my door after school. I opened the door to find Caitlyn, who quickly came in and made herself at home. After getting a quick hug and catching up on all the news, I asked her why she stopped by. She said, "Mrs. Spencer, I need one of those dinosaur books for my English class, and I was hoping that you could tell me where to get one." "Dinosaur books," I asked, stumped. "I don't know what dinosaur book you're talking about." "You know, the dinosaur books we used in resource. You know the one. Here—they're right here on this shelf!" Caitlyn proceeded to take me over to the class library and pointed out the "dinosaur book" that she was looking for. It was the thesaurus. Bronto**saurus**—the**saurus**. Caitlyn had used her knowledge of word roots to infer that a thesaurus was somehow related to dinosaurs! I was actually quite impressed, and from then on, in my classroom we always called the thesaurus "The Dinosaur Book."*

Using Context Clues

Another powerful strategy for acquiring and understanding new vocabulary is context clues. The CCSS identify this skill as a critical one from Grade 1 on up through high school (L.1.4.A – L.11-12.4.A). This skill needs to be taught explicitly over time and needs to be developed from simple strategies, such as comprehending the general idea (Grades 1–3) or learning different types of context clues (Grades 4 and 5) to more sophisticated strategies such as using a word's position and grammatical function to help determine meaning (Grades 6–12). There are several different types of context clues that have been identified and taught in different curricula, and they aren't always the same. Table 6.2 shows you four commonly taught types of context clues.

Figures 6.1 and 6.2 show examples of the types of graphic organizers that might be used to help students learn to interpret context clues for vocabulary. UDL asks us to provide alternate representations of new information, so we would want to provide good, clear instruction and modeling of the use of the four types of context clues before using these organizers. Interested in representing this information in yet another way? Check out this video for an entertaining alternative: www.flocabulary.com/context-clues. (The authors of that video gave away their age when they included Perry Mason in the lyrics, but I still think it's a fun and engaging way to get kids to interact with these ideas.)

Table 6.2 Commonly Taught Types of Context Clues

Type of Context Clue	What It Is	Example
Definition	The definition of the word is actually given in the sentence.	*Josh thought her dress was* **elegant***; in other words, he thought it was sophisticated and stylishly graceful.*
Synonym	Another word (or words) with the same meaning is included in the sentence or paragraph.	*To the old man, the movie was* **preposterous.** *He found it absurd!*
Antonym	Another word (or words) with the opposite meaning is given that helps define the word.	*Sandy was* **incredulous** *when she first heard the news, but later on she began to understand that it was actually true.*
Examples or Inference	The meaning has to be figured out or inferred from the information or examples given.	*The meal was* **colossal***, so everyone was completely stuffed when they were done eating.*

The website of the International Reading Association, recently renamed as the International Literacy Association (www.readwritethink .org), offers a variety of vocabulary lesson plans that involve students in learning new vocabulary. One strategy they recommend is combining the teaching of context clues with semantic gradients (sometimes referred to as shades of meaning) to help students understand the relationships between words with similar meanings (Greenwood & Flanigan, 2007). For example, you might first teach your students how to use context to infer the meaning of the bold word in the following sentence: *Her husband was* **meticulous** *in his planning, so they had no problems during their trip.* Then you can use a semantic gradient to explore other words that would fit within that sentence, and discuss how each would change the meaning.

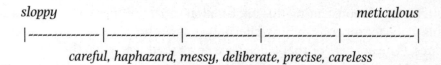

sloppy   *meticulous*

|--------------|--------------|--------------|--------------|--------------|

careful, haphazard, messy, deliberate, precise, careless

Source: Adapted from ReadWriteThink.org.

Figure 6.1 Searching for Context Clues!

Report by Detective _____

I am on the case at midnight, on this date: _____, when I stumble upon the following sentence:

Wait! There is a word in that sentence I don't understand! Thinking quickly, I underline the pesky word in red ink. There, that's better. Now at least I have identified the scoundrel!

I pull my magnifying glass from my pocket and carefully examine the sentence for clues—*CONTEXT CLUES!* Using my excellent prior knowledge, I collect my clues, using these handy boxes to organize them.

Definition	Synonym	Antonym	Examples/Inference

My superior powers of detection have not failed me!! I now know that this word means:

Figure 6.2 Searching for Context Clues!

Name: _____

Sentence:

Definition/ Example	Synonym	Antonym	Examples/ Inference

The definition is actually given in the sentence. EG: He **perused** the crime scene, **looking closely for clues**.

Another word in the sentence has the same meaning. EG: **The petrified man was so scared he was shaking.**

Another word in the sentence has the opposite meaning. EG: Sharon **was illiterate, but her brother was a good reader.**

Word meanings have to be inferred from the sentence. EG: **Jose was inundated with email, so it took him all day to answer them.**

Meaning:

How I figured it out:

Here are two more fun ways to use shades of meaning. Gather paint samples from a hardware store, and use them to display synonyms in order of intensity.

 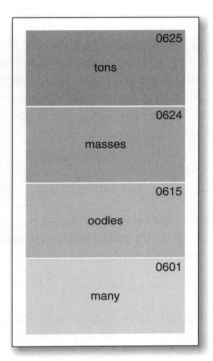

Another interactive way to explore synonyms is with a synonym timeline. In this activity, your students kinesthetically put synonyms in order of intensity by hanging them on a clothesline. Give students the opportunity to work with a partner when they try this one as the discussion is a huge part of the learning. Shades of meaning are identified in the Common Core writing standards in kindergarten and continue as a focus through third grade (L.K.5.D – L.3.5.C).

Source: Adapted from Hougan (2006).

Sally's After Lunch Strategy. One more quick strategy for helping students explore synonyms is what I like to call the "after lunch" strategy. I believe that every teacher should do this strategy every day, right after lunch, for five minutes. It only takes a couple of minutes of preparation, but by the end of the school year, you can expose your students to more than 500 new words with this one simple activity. If you are a high school content teacher, do it with content vocabulary; this strategy can work for just about everyone.

To create this activity, write a sentence on the board with a word missing. Underneath, give three possibilities of words that could fit into the blank. Then hold a discussion about why an author might choose one word over the other.

The mailman was _____ *when the dog jumped out and bit him.*
            afraid, startled, upset

The constable was _____ *by the horrendous driving he observed*
            appalled, aghast, stupefied
on New Year's Eve.

Source: Adapted from McCormick (2006).

You will be amazed (or aghast, or stupefied!) by the quality of conversation you can generate just by implementing this simple strategy every day. Before long, students will be immersing themselves in discussion about the similarities and differences of each of the three words, exploring ways they can change the meaning of the sentence through their choices. Have students discuss in pairs or small groups before sharing with the class to engage the more reluctant learners. This five-minute after-lunch strategy can pack a huge punch in the classroom!

Figurative Language

Alliteration

Two turtles
taking turns

Figurative language is introduced in the CC writing standards in third grade and continues as an area of focus all the way into twelfth grade (L.3.5 – L.11-12.5). Pictures and cartoons can be used as powerful tools to help students understand figurative language. I really like these figurative language posters by Laura Torres (available at http://www.teacherspayteachers.com/Store/Laura-Torres). Laura has created a variety of fun, student-friendly posters to represent the most common types of figurative language in a way that almost any student can understand.

Many teachers like to identify and study an idiom of the week, and several companies have created materials to support that idea. ReadWriteThink.org has an interactive online idiom unit called Eye on Idioms that allows students to explore a variety of idioms with picture supports. They can print out their work to turn in on completion, but it can't be saved online (http://www.readwritethink .org/files/resources/interactives/idioms/).

Like other components of language that we've discussed in this chapter, for students to master figurative language and idioms, they need multiple opportunities to interact with them in a variety of contexts over time. Whenever possible, make the instruction lively and kinesthetic (act out the idiom!), build in lots of repetition, and use visual supports to help make these tricky elements of the Common Core language standards more accessible to your students. Here are a few more fun ideas: (1) have students pair up to make their own idiom posters; (2) have them practice changing similes into metaphors and vice versa; or (3) play matching games to build in more practice. Kagan's "Who Am I" strategy would be a fun one to use here. Students have idioms written on cards and taped to their backs, and they rove around the room, asking for clues to help them guess their idiom (Kagan & Kagan, 2009).

Integrating Vocabulary Knowledge Into Writing

After you've spent all of this time helping your students learn and practice new vocabulary, sometimes when they write, they end up using the same old words. How do you help them integrate the new vocabulary words into their writing? Unfortunately, there's no magic answer, but there are a few quick strategies that can increase the likelihood that they will be able to actually use all the vocabulary that you've been so assiduously teaching them. First, think back to Chapter 1. One of the big deals about writing is that students have to do so many things at once; and one of the most problematic things for students with disabilities is spelling. Many kids with disabilities end up using very simple vocabulary because those are the only words they know how to spell. Personal dictionaries, word boxes, and word walls can all help remediate that problem; so can brainstorming vocabulary before students write. Letting reluctant spellers brainstorm words into a speech-to-text device such as Siri is a wonderful way to create individualized word lists before students write. You might also consider letting them brainstorm in pairs or small groups, which will provide more support to those students who have trouble recalling vocabulary because of memory deficits.

One final trick is something I've learned myself as I've grown older and my word recall has started to lag. Many times as I was writing this book, I wanted to use a particular word but just couldn't recall it. It would be right on the tip of my tongue, but if I sat there trying to remember it, all my ideas and productivity would come to a screeching halt. What I've learned to do is type a line in the position where the word will go, then move on. For example, if I were trying to recall the word *position* in the previous sentence, I would type, "What I've learned to do is type a line in the _____ where the word will go." I've discovered that I can come back to it several sentences later, and the word will almost always appear from my subconscious like magic. For me, this strategy is almost foolproof, so I urge you to have your students try it and let me know how it goes. At the very least, they won't slow down their workflow trying to think of that one special word.

Be really judicious with your use of the dictionary in the classroom: research has shown that because of the complexity of the language in most dictionaries (even children's dictionaries), struggling learners will have trouble using them effectively (Beck, McKeown, & Kucan, 2013). Consider purchasing the COBUILD Dictionaries, *published by Collins. They are specifically written to be accessible to a wide range of learners and use clear, simple sentences to define words. For example, here is the definition of the word* **wag** *from dictionary.com: "***wag:*** to move from side to side, forward and back, up and down." Here is the definition from the COBUILD Advanced Dictionary: "When a dog* **wags** *its tail, it repeatedly waves its tail from side to side." You can see how that second definition would be much more comprehensible for most students. There are several different editions of COBUILD, including a Primary Learner's Dictionary for primary students whose first language is not English. They can be purchased at Amazon or on the Collins website, www.collins.co.uk.* Many different versions of the COBUILD Dictionary *are also available as apps.*

Clarifying Syntax

The COBUILD online dictionary defines syntax as "the ways that words can be put together, or are put together, in order to make sentences." In other words, syntax requires students to break down and understand how the different parts of a sentence come together to make meaning. This can be tricky for all of us—if you've ever spent time in classes where they like to diagram sentences, you know how incredibly complicated it can get! For students with language deficits and disabilities this is one of the most difficult areas to master, and one in which they get all tied up when trying to comprehend text. In particular, many students struggle to understand pronouns and to tie them back to the noun they are replacing. Take a look at this passage from *Alice's Adventures in Wonderland*.

> There was a table set out under the tree in front of the house, and the March Hare and the Hatter were having tea at it. A Dormouse was sitting between them, fast asleep, and the other two were using it as a cushion, resting their elbows on it, and talking over its head. "Very uncomfortable for the Dormouse," thought Alice, "only, as it's asleep, I suppose it doesn't mind." (Carroll, 1865/n.d., p. 90)

The pronoun usage in this text is very complex and would be problematic for many students. "The March Hare and the Hatter were having tea at it." At what? The tree? The house? " . . . the other two were using it as a cushion." Using what? The table? For many of our students with comprehension problems, a paragraph such as this is like a maze and one in which they get irretrievably and permanently lost. Yet these are just the types of intricate sentences we want our more advanced writers to be able to construct.

Simplifying and Expanding Sentences

Beginning as early as third grade, the Common Core language standards ask students to master complex and compound sentences (L.3.1.I) and to use coordinating and subordinating conjunctions to create them. For some students, moving beyond simple sentences to more sophisticated language structures can be challenging well into high school.

LiteracyTA.com has some really good materials for breaking down the parts of complex sentences, and they do so in a visually coherent manner (http://www.literacyta.com/sites/default/files/skill-in-action/7099/writingtypes.pdf). They use clear visual depictions, including color and a coding system, to illustrate this information in a manner that makes it accessible to a wide range of learners. Students are taught that IC stands for independent clause, CC for coordinating conjunction, AC for adverbial clause, and SC for subordinating conjunction. As the ideas get more complex, the visual representations remain consistent and comprehensible.

One of the elements that secondary teachers sometimes overlook is the importance of students being able to write a good, clear, simple sentence before they can learn to join them together to make complex and compound sentences. For many of our struggling writers, this is a place where their foundational skills may be lacking. For those students, you will need to spend time helping them break down their long, run-on sentences into clear, simple sentences first; then they can progress to using conjunctions to join them together into more complex structures. Don't

be surprised if some students (particularly those with learning disabilities) have to go back to this foundational step multiple times, sometimes well into middle and high school, before they master it.

Supporting Decoding

In order to write, students first have to gather information, and most of the time that requires reading. No matter what grade you are teaching, please don't assume that your students with disabilities can access text easily, even when it is online or digital. Many of your students may need support to help them simply decode the text. What follows are a few of my favorite tools to help students access printed text.

- *Bookshare.* Bookshare is a tool that was created through a grant from the Office of Special Education Programs in Washington, D.C. Bookshare is the world's largest online library of digital texts for individuals with print disabilities, and it is available for free to students who qualify. The tools and resources are too many for me to list here, but I encourage you to check it out at www.bookshare.org. If you have students with disabilities in your classes, you should get them access to Bookshare.
- *Learning Ally.* Learning Ally is another online source for audiobooks, specifically targeted for students with print disabilities. Like Bookshare, you can only buy a membership to Learning Ally if you have a documented disability. Learning Ally is not free but is reasonably priced for most families and classrooms. Visit https://www.learningally.org.
- *Readability.* For many of our students (not just those with disabilities), the Internet can be overwhelming. You open a page to explore new information and find yourself bombarded by ads, banners, links, and a lot of other stuff that only serves as a distraction from the information you are trying to uncover. I think Readability is one of the best tools around for dealing with this problem, and it's a free download. Readability takes a cluttered webpage and converts it into a clean, simple page with only the primary information visible to your readers. It's like magic! You can download Readability for the browser(s) you most frequently use, and once you have it, you'll wonder how you ever lived without it. Take a look at the pictures below for an example: the one on the left is a page from the San Diego Zoo website before Readability. On the right is what comes up with one click of the Readability browser button. Although the second version may look more boring to you, for students who need help focusing, this is an invaluable tool.

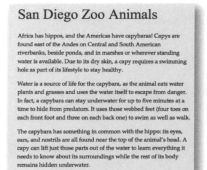

- *Web Reader for iPads.* iPads come with a built-in readability feature in Safari. When you are browsing the web in Safari on your iPad, look for the little text icon on the left hand side of the browser window. Click on that, and Safari will automatically simplify the text for you, just as Readability does in the computer environment. Below is an example of a webpage before and after clicking the web reader icon in Safari for iPad. (FYI, it doesn't show up in all websites, but it does in many.) You can also get a Readability app for your tablet if the web-reader feature doesn't suffice.

Illustrating Through Multiple Media

In most classrooms, text is the primary mode of learning. But as we have mentioned before, text is not an effective tool for all students, particularly those that have language-based disabilities. I have sprinkled ideas for using other forms of representation throughout this chapter, but here are a few more that I don't want to leave out!

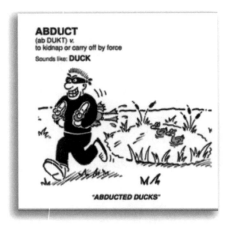

• *Vocabulary Cartoons*

I am a huge fan of the Vocabulary Cartoons books created by Sam Burchers (2007). There are three different levels available, as well as DVDs and other materials. The cartoons use the key-word strategy to help students associate the new word with one they already know. You can see it at work in the elementary sample shown here. You can purchase the materials through their website at www.vocabularycartoons.com or get the books on Amazon.

• LINCS Strategy

Ed Ellis and the folks at the University of Kansas developed a strategy for learning vocabulary that has been tested multiple times with students with disabilities and which has been shown to help them understand and retain complex words over time. Much like Vocabulary Cartoons, the LINCS strategy (Ellis, 1992) asks students to use a linking or key word to help them create a mental representation of the new word's meaning. Students are taught to create a short story to link the key word to the new word, draw a picture that illustrates the link, and write a definition in their own words.

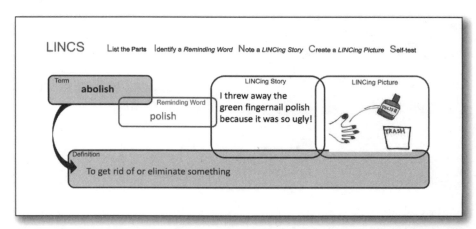

Source: Copyright © Edwin S. Ellis. The LINCS Vocabulary Strategy. www.MakesSenseStrategies.com

The LINCS program is available through the Interactive LINCS software package, available at www.graphicorganizers.com. There are many other fabulous resources from Dr. Ellis also available at that site.

GUIDELINE #6: PROVIDING OPTIONS FOR PERCEPTION

The final guideline for representation involves student perception. This guideline asks us to consider the following critical question: Are our students able to take in and process the materials we are using to teach them? Many of our students struggle with perceptual difficulties, vision problems, decreased or inability to hear, and other physical and cognitive factors that can make it difficult for them to attend to and process a "typical" teacher-led lesson. Luckily, there are some easy tweaks we can make in our classrooms so it is a little bit easier for *all* our students to succeed.

Display of Information

When you are teaching your students to write, think carefully about the way you visually present the instruction. Below are a couple of strategies that can help you ensure that you are making your teaching as accessible as possible when you display information.

- *Consider color.* Some students have trouble visually processing high-contrast handouts and graphics. Consider using pastel colored paper for handouts, and try a variety of colors on materials and the whiteboard to see what suits your students best. Some of your students may have an easier time writing on colored paper as well. (Here's a useful tip: let students use different colors of paper for different drafts to help them keep track of their progress.) In general, choose colors that reflect less light and avoid using colors together that are adjacent to each other on the spectrum, such as blue print on green paper (Griffin, Williams, Davis, & Engleman, 2002). A colleague with a visual disability shared that Arial font in black, no smaller than twelve point, makes it much easier for her to read.
- *Cursive writing.* Many students with reading problems have a great deal of difficulty decoding cursive handwriting. This is particularly true in elementary school, where many below-average readers are still struggling to decode simple printing. If you have students in your classroom who are decoding below about the fourth-grade level, you might consider switching from cursive writing to printing to make the writing more accessible to everyone.
- *Print size and layout.* For poor readers, the size and density of text on a page can have a significant impact (Hughes & Wilkins, 2000). Whether you are presenting sample essays for students to analyze

or creating graphic organizers for planning, consider leaving plenty of white space on the page and using a font size that is large enough to avoid intimidating reluctant readers.

- *Slow down!* One of the simplest "fixes" for the inclusive classroom is just to slow down your rate of speech. For students with attention difficulties, auditory processing difficulties, or hearing impairment, a slower rate of speech can make all the difference. Emphasize clarity, and choose a rate of speech that gives students time to process. Need a model? Search out an old episode of *Mr. Rogers' Neighborhood*; Mr. Rogers knew exactly the right pace to make his speech accessible to viewers of all ages. (You don't have to change your shoes, though . . .)

ALTERNATIVES TO AUDITORY AND VISUAL INFORMATION

Let's be honest. Most of us rely on our voices for the vast majority of our teaching. However, if you are teaching mostly with your voice, you may be leaving behind a big chunk of your student audience, even if you don't have students who are deaf or hard of hearing in your classes. (If you do, then of course you need to make accommodations for those students.) As I have mentioned previously, many students have difficulty processing speech and need more time, as well as visual supports, to help them make sense of what their teachers are saying. On the other hand, the visual tools you are using may not be accessible if you have students with visual impairments in your class. Consider some of the following tips to make your instruction more accessible to all your learners:

- *Create synchronized visual and auditory supports.* I recently attended a wonderful professional development workshop for teachers where the trainer was recommending using music as a cue for classroom management. It was a terrific idea, but my first thought was, "What about the deaf students?" After some serious ruminating, I came up with the idea of using a simultaneous video. When the teacher puts on the eighty-second music cue to signal the transition to lunch, she can also use her computer to play an eighty-second video, such as the opening credits from *The Simpsons*, to cue the students who can't hear the music. When they see that the video is almost over, they know their transition time is also almost at an end.

- *Provide text for your visuals.* I've mentioned the importance of visual supports throughout this book, but it can't hurt to mention them again. John Medina, the author of the wonderful book *Brain Rules*, states simply that "vision trumps everything" (2014). Providing charts, graphics, pictures, etc. will help almost every student in your room make more sense of what they hear. But for your students with visual disabilities, you need to give them access to the same tools. When

you insert a picture, graph, or illustration into a document, make sure you provide alternative text so that screen readers can make sense of it. Here you can see an example. This is a picture of my adorable puppy Cherry when she was about a week old. Say it with me: "AWWWWW . . . " After I inserted the picture, I right-clicked on it, chose "Format Picture," and then chose "Alt Text." I inserted the following text: *Title: Picture of Baby Cherry. Description: This is an adorable picture of my puppy Cherry when she was about a week old. It shows her little black and white face being cradled in the arms of her foster mom, with her tiny tongue sticking out.* When you create alt text, you want to try to capture the feeling of the picture through the text as much as possible. You always need to include a title—the screen reader reads the title first, allowing the user to choose whether they want or need to hear the whole description. This same principle applies to giving verbal descriptions of visuals you use in the classroom. Trust me—having had students with visual disabilities in my classes, I know how hard it can be to remember to provide them these types of supports. But over time, if you persevere, you will find yourself giving beautiful verbal descriptions of the visuals in your class. It will not only help your students with visual deficits, but it will be a great language-development tool for all your students.
- *Use captions and descriptions.* Video can be an amazing tool, and there are lots of good videos out there that can enhance your teaching of the Common Core writing standards. (There are also lots of bad ones, too, so I urge you to choose carefully!) However, always remember to caption your videos so they are accessible to all your students. If your video isn't captioned, try the YouTube self-captioning system. Click on the CC symbol at the bottom of a video

to turn them on. Often the self-generated captions are inaccurate, though, so preview them first, and provide corrections to your students where needed. Clicking on the "transcript" button below the video shows the captions with time codes—you can copy and paste this into a Word document if you want to provide a written transcript for students. If your videos have a lot of places where there is no text, you will want to supplement this written transcript with descriptions of the action for your students with visual disabilities. Sadly, this only works with YouTube videos you "own"; for others you will have to live with the automatic captioning.

- *Speech to text.* One of my favorite ways to use an iPhone is as an assistive device for communicating with individuals who are deaf. This isn't the ideal way to communicate, of course, but if you don't know ASL and need to communicate with a deaf person, Siri can be a really helpful tool. Open the Notes app, start a new page, then use the dictation button (circled in red in the picture) to convert your speech into text. I've used it multiple times to communicate in stores and in our school offices as well as to interact with students when there isn't an interpreter at hand. Obviously, other phones have similar tools. The point is that we have amazing assistive devices in our pockets much of the time, and we shouldn't be afraid to use them in our classrooms.

- *Use realia.* One of the most engaging writing lessons I've experienced was done several years ago by a fifth-grade teacher I know. She was working on descriptive writing with her students, and she noticed that their descriptions tended to be very stale and one-dimensional. To help them get a grasp of what they were really capable of, she created a "sensory picnic" in her classroom. One day when her students came into the room, they found it covered in photographs of a picnic in a park. The students all walked around the room and discussed the pictures for a few minutes, generating memories of picnics they had been on. Then she had them all sit down at their tables and put on blindfolds, and she proceeded to guide them through a series of sensory experiences to help them imagine a picnic. She turned on a fan to create a breeze in the classroom and had them taste watermelon and fried chicken. They ran their hands over a picnic basket and tree branches and sniffed at charcoal and newly mown grass. In the background, she played a recording of children laughing and playing, with the sounds of dogs barking and birds chirping. In about fifteen minutes, each student had experienced a picnic through all five of their senses, and the descriptive essays they subsequently wrote were rich with the descriptive detail she had provided for them. Although there were no students with visual or hearing impairments in her class, if there had been, they would have each had a vivid experience very much like all the other students. This teacher had created a lesson that was not only accessible for students with a variety of learning challenges, but she had built an immersive experience that helped every student in the room understand the complexity of descriptive writing in a very personal way.

I suspect some of you are feeling overwhelmed right now. I've been there—I know it can be daunting to consider making everything accessible to everyone. The truth is, though, it becomes easier with practice, and every time you create alternative means of expression, you are building a bank of materials that you can use again and again. And remember, you don't have to be perfect right away. A year ago, I was overwhelmed by the idea of adding alternate text to all my pictures—now it's second nature and a very quick process. The more you think about your classroom in terms of *providing options* that are designed to support all your students, the more this will become ingrained in your teaching practice. Before you know it, you will have a universally designed classroom where practically every

Table 6.3   Accessible Apps for Students Who Need More Support in Writing

Application	Description	Cost
Same Meaning Magic	An adventure game designed to help individuals understand synonyms.	**$0.99**
Montessori Crosswords	A phonics game that helps to develop reading, writing, and spelling skills by building words from a set of 320 word-image-audio-phonics combinations using a phonics-enabled movable alphabet.	**$2.99**
PaperPort Notes	A digital note-taking tool for the iPad that allows the combination of documents, Web content, audio, typed text, as well as handwritten notes into a single document.	**Free**
Tools4 Students	Offers twenty-five graphic organizers for students to use to support and organize their thinking while reading or preparing to write. Covers common comprehension skills: cause/effect, main idea/detail, sequence events, pro/con, story elements, characterization, word meaning, plot, compare and contrast, etc.	**$0.99**

(Continued)

Table 6.3 (Continued)

Application	Description	Cost
Rocket Speller	An entertaining game where the player chooses rocket pieces needed to build a custom rocket ship and spells words to fuel it. Place letters in order. Audible and visual hints are given when needed to place letters in the correct order.	**Free**
Grammar Jammers	Animated songs, rhymes, and quiz questions on grammar usage and mechanics.	**Free**
iBooks	Download and read fully illustrated and multi-touch books filled with interactive features. Choose from different fonts, brightnesses, and page colors. Use accessibility features in iPad, iPhone, and iPod Touch, such as speaking the words on a given page.	**Free**
Interactive Alphabet	Learn letters and sounds through interactive play. Flashcards with text, images, and sound. Reads the text, including the letter sound. A mode can be activated to automatically turn pages.	**Free**
iWordQ CA	A Canadian English app that supports writers and readers. In writing mode, a text editor is used with word-prediction support, spell-check and dictionary access, and speech recognition.	**$24.99**
Symbol Support	Words can be translated into pictures and symbols. Symbols (over 6,000 photos or images from the Internet) and speech to text can be added to documents. Text is highlighted word by word. Documents created in SymbolSupport can also be read with the free SymbolReader app.	$39.99

lesson is rich with visual, auditory, and kinesthetic options that immerse your students in the curriculum and provide pathways to understanding for all types of learners.

WRAPPING UP THE BIG IDEAS

- Learning Latin and Greek roots helps students make connections between vocabulary words they already know and new ones.
- Students should be explicitly taught how to use context clues to make meaning of unfamiliar words.

- Visual supports, such as semantic gradients (for synonyms) and picture supports for figurative language, can help students synthesize and comprehend the new information.
- Students need to be taught how to break down complex syntax in their reading and how to apply that to their writing.
- There are a variety of web-based tools and apps that can help students with print disabilities access text for research when they are writing.
- Teachers need to develop the habit of presenting information in visual and auditory forms in order to make it accessible to all learners.
- It takes time at first, but once you make it a habit, you'll have a classroom that is universally designed for all your students!

FOR FURTHER READING

Beck, I. L., McKeown, M. G., & Kucan, L. (2013). *Bringing words to life* (2nd ed.). New York, NY: Guilford.

Kagan, S., & Kagan, M. (2009). *Kagan Cooperative Learning.* San Clemente, CA: Kagan Publishing.

Rasinski, T., Padak, N., Newton, R. M., & Newton, E. (2008). *Greek & Latin roots: Keys to building vocabulary.* Huntington Beach, CA: Shell Education.

Action and Expression

7

Let students play to their strengths, not to their weaknesses.
Let them show what they can do, not what they can't.
Give them the opportunity to celebrate their gifts and talents.
Help your students shine!

I magine that you are about to take an intensive test to show that you are capable of being a good teacher. No worries! You have all the knowledge and skills you need to pass that test, and you would probably enter the testing room feeling confident, right? Now imagine that you sit down to take the test and it's written in French. Sure, you had several years of French back in high school, but you certainly don't remember enough to read and interpret academic questions. How are you supposed to pass a test that's written in a language in which you have no fluency? Despite your best efforts, at the end of that exam you will probably be frustrated and exhausted, and the examiners will have no idea whether you really have the teaching skills they were testing.

Congratulations! You've just experienced what it's like to be a student with a learning difference. The truth is that many exams and assignments are not testing what our students with disabilities know; they are testing their disabilities. Let me say that again: **we aren't always assessing what they know; we may be assessing their disabilities.** This is a heartbreaking state of affairs that not only disengages the students from academics but leaves teachers without the information they need to be effective. The formats of many tests and assignments are such that students with learning challenges can't overcome their limitations to demonstrate what they really know or understand.

The following quote is a perfect description of this conundrum. It's often attributed to Einstein, but it seems that no one is really sure who said it first. Nevertheless, it's a great sentiment and applies perfectly to the UDL principle of action and expression:

> *If you judge a fish by its ability to climb a tree, it will live its whole life believing that it is stupid.*

This quote speaks to the very heart of this third principle of UDL: how do we give all our students the opportunity to show us what they can do? The principle of action and expression is focused on removing the barriers that might cause a student to be unable to demonstrate what he or she really knows about a subject, and the guidelines focus on three areas: developing executive functioning, providing options for expression and communication, and removing barriers to physical action. We will briefly look at these three guidelines here.

Options for Executive Functions

Executive functions are those skills and behaviors that allow us to oversee, regulate, and organize our work. For some young people, what holds them back is not what they know or don't know; it's their inability to manage themselves and their environment as they try to demonstrate their understanding. This guideline asks us to help students develop their skills in planning and goal-setting as we simultaneously lower the dependency on working memory that can stymie the efforts of so many of our young people.

Options for Expression and Communication

Are your students great storytellers? Do they express themselves well through art or dance? How can they best demonstrate what they know? This guideline helps us remove the obstacles that may be holding students back from fully communicating their understanding and urges us to give them opportunities to shine through alternative modes of expression.

Options for Physical Action

Typical classroom materials may be inaccessible to many students. Sometimes, even the technology we use isn't accessible to all our students.

This guideline asks us to be aware of how our students are physically interacting with the curricular materials and to find ways to ensure that all of them truly have equal access.

GUIDELINE #7: SUPPORTING EXECUTIVE FUNCTIONS

The National Center for Learning Disabilities defines executive function as follows: "Executive function is a set of mental processes that helps connect past experience with present action. People use it to perform activities such as planning, organizing, strategizing, paying attention to and remembering details, and managing time and space." Executive function affects almost everything we do throughout our lives. It is what allows us to organize and manage our lives and what helps us keep going under difficult circumstances. The objective of this guideline—supporting executive functions—is to help our students become experts at managing their own learning. Teaching students these skills can make a difference in students' academic careers for a long, long time.

Paige was my student from third to fifth grade, and she was a unique individual. First of all, she was adorable. She had the ability to charm the pants off of anyone around her . . . when she wanted to. But Paige also had some terrific challenges. She was what we sometimes call **twice-exceptional***; she was highly intelligent and had been identified as gifted, but she also had dyslexia and ADHD, which made it very hard for her to decode grade-level materials and to pay attention in the classroom. As a result, Paige was a teacher's worst nightmare. She was disruptive in class, failing most of her subjects, and resistant to the curriculum. She spent a lot of her time in my resource room "recovering" from bad experiences in her general education classes.*

Like most kids, however, Paige really wanted to do better, so she and I worked very hard on developing strategies to help her succeed in the general education classroom. Some of them were small, simple accommodations; for example, we moved her seat to the back of the room and gave her permission to get up and walk around in the back (as long as she didn't disturb other kids). That was very helpful to Paige, who could attend much better when she was in motion. She also learned how to use a graphic organizer for writing—that was terrifically helpful to her in all her subjects. In fact, when she went to middle school, she took multiple copies of the organizer with her so that she could continue to use it, and her mother reported that it was effective for her for many years. In addition, she practiced and mastered some study skills that worked for her unique combination of strengths.

As we tried out these different strategies, Paige learned what worked for her and what didn't, and before long, Paige was an expert on Paige's learning. She became so clear about her own learning strengths and needs that she was a proficient advocate for herself when she got into high school. By building Paige's executive-function skills, we had set her on the path of becoming an expert learner.

Setting Goals

Many students (no matter the grade level) don't know how to set goals, or if they do, their goals tend to be very general and unhelpful. Most young people don't have the skills they need to break a large task into smaller components and set intermediary goals; in fact, this remains an area of challenge for many college students. Yet for most of us, this is exactly the process we need to follow to accomplish long-term or multistep projects. In the next section, we will look at strategies for teaching students to set two different types of goals in writing—short-term goals for day-to-day work and long-term goals to manage more extensive projects.

Setting Short-Term Goals

We have known for years that students who set short-term goals for their work feel more in control and have more confidence about their ability to successfully complete the task (Schunk, 1985). This is especially true in populations of students with learning challenges. Short-term goals are immediate—in other words, "What do I plan to complete today?" Teaching students to set short-term goals before they write will help make the process explicit for them; before they begin to work, they will need to think about the steps in the writing process, identify where they are in that process, and focus on what they should do next. This kind of process-oriented thinking is very helpful to students who struggle with executive function.

Researchers and practitioners often break the writing process down into five steps: **prewriting, drafting, revising, editing,** and **publishing** (see Figure 7.1). These steps provide a great starting point for students who need to set short-term goals; however, for those students who really struggle with executive functioning, it's advisable to break these steps down even more. Figures 7.2, 7.3, and 7.4 provide a view of these five steps divided up into smaller subcomponents, targeted to different age levels. To be most effective, you will probably want to print the steps out on a chart or handout for the students to refer to before they set their goal each day. They should look back at what they did previously, identify where they

Figure 7.1 Steps of the Writing Process

Prewriting. In this step students brainstorm ideas, decide on a topic, and gather research. For older students, a clear thesis statement is generated.

Drafting. In the drafting phase, students write down their ideas, organizing them around a structure such as a paragraph, multiple paragraphs, or claims and counter-claims.

Revising. In the revision step, students review their content and work to make it better. This step is discriminated from the next one by focus on *content* rather than mechanics.

Editing. Now the focus shifts to mechanics, and students need to fix errors in spelling, punctuation, grammar, syntax, etc.

Publishing. The publishing step allows students to share their work through activities such as hanging it on the wall, doing read-alouds or author's chair, or publishing in an online blog or class website.

are in the process, and create a specific goal for the day's work. This strategy can be effective with kids of all ages; as they mature, they will develop goals with more sophistication and deeper insight into their own strengths and needs.

Although your students may not use each of the bullets on these check sheets every time they write, and although the substeps may not be done in this exact order, this type of list makes the process much less ambiguous to students who struggle with executive function. Feel free to modify these lists to the specific demands of the writing task you are teaching or the specific student—in fact, one of the best ways to help students learn to generalize this type of strategy is to use it, modified as needed, over the course of many different types of writing tasks. I've formatted the bullets as check boxes so you can use it as a check-off sheet to scaffold students' progress through the five steps if you wish.

INSIDER TIPS

You will notice that although most of the subcomponents in these charts get developmentally more difficult, a few do not significantly change. For example, all writing needs a good conclusion, so that component remains across grade levels; the expectation for a good conclusion, however, would change as students progress. In addition, even the secondary version still has "I put my name and date on the paper." I have found that even in college this is still a problem for some students, and it's a critically important skill for students to master if they want to get credit for their work.

Figure 7.2 Steps of the Writing Process: Primary

When I'm Writing

Prewriting

- ☐ I think of lots of ideas.
- ☐ I pick an idea.
- ☐ I think of reasons or details.
- ☐ I organize them in a bubble map.

Drafting

- ☐ I write a topic sentence about my idea.
- ☐ I write at least three reason sentences.
- ☐ I write a sentence at the end to wrap it up.

Revising

- ☐ I read my story out loud to make sure it makes sense.
- ☐ I move things around if I need to.
- ☐ I write more if I need to.
- ☐ I cross things out if I need to.
- ☐ I add order words (like *first, next, last)* if I can.

Editing

- ☐ I check every sentence for capital letters.
- ☐ I check all names for capital letters.
- ☐ I check every sentence for ending punctuation.
- ☐ I circle words that might not be spelled right and try to fix them.
- ☐ I ask a partner to look for mistakes I might have missed.
- ☐ I ask the teacher to check it when I'm done.

Publishing

- ☐ I write, type, or dictate a neat final draft.
- ☐ I check it for mistakes and fix them if I can.
- ☐ I make sure my name and the date are on the final draft.
- ☐ I add pictures if I can.
- ☐ I read it to a friend, to the class, or to my parents.

Figure 7.3 Steps of the Writing Process: Upper Elementary

The Writing Process

Prewriting

☐ Brainstorm at least ten ideas or topics.
☐ Choose the idea/topic I like best.
☐ Turn my topic into a complete sentence.
☐ Brainstorm supporting details or reasons.
☐ Choose a graphic organizer that fits my topic.
☐ Organize my ideas in the graphic organizer.

Drafting

☐ Plan out my paragraph(s).
☐ Create a topic sentence for each of my paragraphs.
☐ Draft my supporting ideas into sentences in each paragraph.
☐ Write a transition between each paragraph.
☐ Write a conclusion for the essay.

Revising

☐ Read my essay out loud to make sure it makes sense.
☐ Highlight areas that don't make sense or that need changing.
☐ Rearrange the sentences as needed.
☐ Write more where I don't have enough detail.
☐ Cross things out if they don't fit or don't make sense.
☐ Check the transitions and add or fix them as needed.
☐ Have a partner read it and give me feedback.
☐ Make additional revisions as needed.

Editing

☐ Check every sentence for capital letters.
☐ Check all names for capital letters.
☐ Check every sentence for ending punctuation.
☐ Circle words that might not be spelled right and try to fix them.
☐ Ask a partner to look for mistakes I might have missed.
☐ Ask the teacher to check it when I'm done.

Publishing

☐ Write, type, or dictate a neat final draft.
☐ Check it for mistakes and correct them.
☐ Make sure my name and the date are on the final draft.
☐ Add pictures or illustrations where appropriate.
☐ Read it to a friend, to the class, or to my parents, or publish it online.

Figure 7.4 Steps of the Writing Process: Secondary

The Writing Process

Prewriting

- ☐ Prepare my materials and workspace.
- ☐ Narrow my topic and clearly define it.
- ☐ Research supporting ideas or arguments.
- ☐ Choose an organizing tool that fits my topic, such as an outline, list, or mind map.
- ☐ Organize my ideas in the tool and elaborate on them.
- ☐ Create a timeline for completion of the project.

Drafting

- ☐ Translate my ideas from the organizing tool to a rough outline.
- ☐ Draft my ideas into main sections and paragraphs.
- ☐ Elaborate by including supporting ideas, reasons, or arguments.
- ☐ Write transitions between sections and paragraphs.
- ☐ Write a conclusion.

Revising

- ☐ Read each section out loud a couple of times to make sure it makes sense.
- ☐ Highlight areas that don't make sense or that need revising.
- ☐ Rearrange the sections as needed.
- ☐ Rearrange the paragraphs within each section as needed.
- ☐ Rearrange and/or revise the sentences within the paragraphs as needed.
- ☐ Write more where I don't have enough detail.
- ☐ Cross things out if they don't fit or don't make sense.
- ☐ Check the transitions and add or fix them as needed.
- ☐ Have a partner read it and get feedback.
- ☐ Reread and revise at least twice.

Editing

- ☐ Use COPS to check for mechanical errors.
- ☐ Circle words that might not be spelled right, and look them up or get assistance.
- ☐ Ask a partner to look for mistakes I might have missed.
- ☐ Reread and edit at least twice.

Publishing

- ☐ Type or dictate a high-quality final draft.
- ☐ Check for mistakes using spelling and grammar checks, and fix as needed.
- ☐ Read the final draft aloud for a final check of accuracy.
- ☐ Add illustrations or graphs where appropriate.
- ☐ Make sure my name and date are on the final draft.
- ☐ Turn it in to the appropriate place by the due date.

Source: Adapted from http://www.studygs.net/writing/prewriting.htm

In some cases, some of the skills may seem a little simple for the age level—for instance, the upper-elementary editing list still says to check every sentence for capital letters and ending punctuation. One might expect that a child in upper elementary would have already mastered those skills, but remember—these lists are designed to meet the needs of the *range* of learners in every class. I have yet to see a fifth-grade classroom that didn't have at least one student who still forgets to capitalize and punctuate appropriately.

In the secondary list, I added the mnemonic device COPS as an editing tool. In my experience, many students still need to be walked through the process of editing for mechanics, even well into high school. The mnemonic **COPS** is a good one for basic mechanics: it was developed by the folks at the University of Kansas and stands for **C**apitalization, **O**verall appearance, **P**unctuation, and **S**pelling. Some people like to change it up a little to add other important skills: I've seen **COPS-SS** (adds on **S**entence **S**tructure to the end) and **STOPS** (**S**entence structure, **T**enses, **O**verall appearance, **P**unctuation, and **S**pelling). You could also make up your own. Remember, whatever mnemonic device you choose, make sure you use the steps of SRSD (Chapter 5, p. 71) to teach it to your students explicitly, and give them lots of opportunities to practice with feedback until they can use it independently.

Setting Long-Term Goals

Long-term goals require students to more deeply analyze their own work and consider their individual learning strengths and challenges. As you can imagine, helping students to do this type of critical scrutiny of their own work can lead to a profound understanding of their learning and, ultimately, to a student who knows how to set up a learning task to suit his or her individual needs.

Long-term goals are best set at the beginning or end of a unit of study. In writing, many teachers will ask students to evaluate their work after finishing a writing task and to set a goal for their next writing assignment. Some students will be able to do this independently, and others will need teacher guidance to choose the goals that will be most helpful to their overall development.

Figures 7.5, 7.6, and 7.7 contain some goal-setting sheets that you may use or modify; again, they are leveled for different ages of students. Beginning at a young age, these sheets are designed to help students analyze their own writing skills and think carefully about a goal based on that analysis.

One semester I had a group of seventh graders, all of whom strug-gled with executive function. Although they tried their hardest in their classes, their inability to organize themselves, to meet deadlines, and to manage their time kept them from being successful. The second half of the year, I made special arrangements to meet with this group for ten minutes at the end of every day, where we spent time discussing how to organize their materials, desks, and study areas at home. We made checklists for their backpacks and created color-coded file folders for all of their different subjects. Then we tackled scheduling, learning how to use an online calendar that they could update from their phones, and we spent several weeks learning and practicing how to backwards-plan big assignments. Finally, we spent about a month learning how to set short- and long-term goals to help them manage the workload across all of their subjects.

I wish I could tell you that I collected data and that it showed great improvement, but in fact, I didn't have the presence of mind to do that. Like you, I was a busy teacher with a lot on my mind. However, what I can tell you is this: about two years later, I was in Costco, and David, one of the students from that group, came up to me with his mom to say hi. Before I could ask him for an update on his life, he blurted out, "Mrs. Spencer? Do you remember that scheduling thing we did in sev-enth grade? That was the best thing I've done in my whole school career. That helped me in high school more than anything else I learned."

When a student values something enough to mention it to a teacher two years later, you know that you've made a significant difference in his life. It turns out that teaching executive-function skills was one of the best things I'd done in MY whole school career, too!

Reducing the Demands on Working Memory

If you think back to Chapter 1, you will remember that working memory is the type of memory that lets you hold information in your head while you complete a task. The cognitive load associated with work-ing memory during writing is very high and causes many students to struggle during writing tasks. In my opinion, one of the most important scaffolds you can give to struggling writers is to reduce the working-memory load; for many students, this can make the act of writing much more manageable and can turn them into able, independent writers. One of the easiest ways to reduce the demands on working memory is by having the students focus on one thing at a time as they go through the steps of the writing process.

Figure 7.5 Writing Goal Sheet: Primary

My Writing Goals

Name:

Things I like about my writing:

- ☐ My topic is clear.
- ☐ My ideas make sense.
- ☐ The sentences are good.
- ☐ I used capital letters.
- ☐ I used punctuation marks.
- ☐ The spelling is good.
- ☐ It has a strong ending.

Things I could do better:

- ☐ My topic
- ☐ My ideas
- ☐ The sentences
- ☐ The capital letters
- ☐ The punctuation marks
- ☐ The spelling
- ☐ The ending

My goal for next time is:

I chose this because:

Who will help me?

- ☐ My teacher
- ☐ My parents
- ☐ My friend

   _____

- ☐ Someone else

   _____

Did I reach my goal?

- ☐ Yes
- ☐ Almost
- ☐ Not yet

Why?

   _____

   _____

Figure 7.6 Writing Goal Sheet: Upper Elementary

My Writing Goals

Name:

My writing strengths:

Things I could improve:

My goal for next time:

I chose this because:

Did I reach my goal?

☐ Yes
☐ Almost
☐ Not yet

Next time I will: _____

_____

_____

Figure 7.7   Writing Goal Sheet: Secondary

Writing Goal Sheet

Name:

Strengths of last essay or paper:

☐ Planning _____

☐ Organizing _____

☐ Developing Ideas _____

☐ Revising/Editing _____

☐ Mechanics _____

Areas for improvement:

☐ Planning _____

☐ Organizing _____

☐ Developing Ideas _____

☐ Revising/Editing _____

☐ Mechanics _____

Goal for next time:

_____

_____

_____

Reason I chose this goal:

_____

_____

_____

Goal met   Goal not met

(circle one)

Reasons/thoughts for next time:

_____

_____

_____

Planning

Ziad is a student with poor working memory, and he struggles with all stages of writing. When Ziad tries to brainstorm ideas, the demands of remembering how to spell words as he quickly generates ideas slows him

down considerably, and many times he forgets the next idea because he's still trying to write down the previous one. To reduce the memory load for Ziad, we need to give him access to tools for recording his thoughts as he brainstorms. That could mean he uses the dictation tool on an iPad to brainstorm or that he dictates his ideas into an old-fashioned tape recorder. It could also mean that he works with a partner to take turns writing down each other's ideas. Any of these options is terrific, and any of them will help Ziad get his ideas on the page before he forgets them. Once Ziad has his ideas on paper, it is an easy next step to transcribe them onto an appropriate organizer.

The more independent you can make your students, the better. So if your students can learn to generate ideas into a speech-to-text tool, like the iPad, they will be able to use this skill for the rest of their lives. Dictating to a peer is a great "gateway" strategy to working without adult help, but ultimately, learning to be proficient with technology is the key to independence for kids with working-memory deficits.

Drafting

Spelling is also one of the biggest villains when it comes to helping students with working-memory deficits draft their ideas. In Chapter 1 we met Raymond, one of my former students with working-memory problems and

very poor spelling skills. Raymond had a spoken vocabulary that was actually above grade level—when you talked to him, you could tell exactly how intelligent he was and how much knowledge he had about multiple subjects. However, Raymond's writing did not reflect any of this; because he couldn't remember how to spell most of the higher-level vocabulary words he knew, Raymond tended to use only very low-level, simple words in his writing. In addition, his fine-motor skills were a bit delayed, so the very act of writing also consumed some of his working-memory capacity. For

Raymond, the opportunity to dictate his writing was crucial—if he was able to "think and speak" rather than "think and write," most of his working-memory problems disappeared. Like Ziad, Raymond could use a speech-to-text tool, a simple recording device, or a peer, and because Raymond was easily bored, he liked to choose different strategies on different days. That was okay with me!

Revising and Editing

Imagine this scenario. You are in your classroom, and Roya comes up to you with a draft of her informational essay on global climate change. You glance down and see that it is riddled with mechanical errors. What do most teachers say at that point? "Go back and edit this carefully—check for spelling errors, punctuation errors, run-on sentences, etc. before you bring it back to me." Unfortunately, if Roya is a young lady with a working-memory deficit, most likely, when she brings it back to you, it won't be much better. When asked to edit for multiple different components, Roya will have trouble holding them all in her working memory, so she will overlook many if not most of her errors as she reads through her work. It's not that she isn't paying attention (although it will no doubt look that way to many people); it's that she literally can't remember all those elements at once, so as she scans her work for spelling errors, she completely forgets about punctuation, capitalization, etc.

For Roya to be successful, she needs to *chunk* the editing into small bits. In other words, she needs to make multiple passes through her work, each one focused on a different component. This is true for the steps of revision (focused on ideas and organization) and for editing (focused on mechanics). I recommend students start with the higher-level skills first, then work their way down to the lower-level details like spelling, using a checklist (or lists) to guide them. At first, Roya will most likely balk at having to read through her essay so many times, but once she sees how successful she can be at improving her writing and reducing the number of red marks from the teacher, she and most other students will adapt to this system over time. Figure 7.8 gives a checklist that can be a starting point for the kids in your classroom—make sure that you adapt it for the specific age of your students and the specific demands of your writing assignments.

Figure 7.8   Action and Expression

Revising/Editing Checklist	Changes Made
REVISING	
☐ I read through once to make sure it made sense.	☐
☐ I read each paragraph again to make sure each was focused on one idea.	☐
☐ I checked each paragraph for a clear topic sentence.	☐
☐ I read through again and circled boring words. I replaced them with more interesting, specific words.	☐
☐ I read through again and looked for short sentences to combine into complex sentences.	☐
☐ I read through to look for run-on sentences.	☐
☐ I read my introduction to see if it captures the reader's attention.	☐
EDITING	
☐ I read through and circled misspelled words to fix them.	☐
☐ I read through again and checked for capital letters in every sentence and on proper nouns.	☐
☐ I read through to check for punctuation in every sentence and quotation marks where needed.	☐
☐ I checked to make sure every paragraph was indented.	☐

Supervise your students carefully at first to make sure that they are actually doing a separate read-through for each element on the checklist; many students will try to "cheat" and do it all at once. As they get more proficient, challenge them to combine two or three elements into one read-through. This will help them develop their working-memory skills and build confidence in their abilities. It's important not to make students do all this in one sitting, particularly at first. Break it up into small chunks of time so the demands of editing for so many different elements don't overwhelm them.

Monitoring Progress

A critical component of executive function requires students to learn how to monitor their progress. This is where a lot of students with learning challenges get in trouble. I immediately think about Aaron, a young man with ADHD who struggled with many of the demands of his classroom. Aaron was constantly getting in trouble because he wasn't on task. He also seemed to lack insight into his own learning strengths and challenges—when asked to correct his work, he frequently became lost and overwhelmed. As a result, Aaron was always in trouble with his teachers; they complained that not only was the quality of his work poor but he didn't care!

The truth was that Aaron cared; in fact, when he was in elementary school, he cared deeply. However, as he progressed through the grades, earning passing marks by the skin of his teeth, he started to resent being accused of not caring, and pretty soon, he began to live up to his teachers' expectations. Eventually, Aaron stopped caring.

In truth, the problem with Aaron was that he had a very difficult time discerning what to do next to improve his work, and he had grown very dependent on adult feedback and direction to guide his classroom behaviors. The following was a typical scenario for Aaron when he was writing: he would finish a draft and bring it up to the teacher for feedback, and she would say something like, "Aaron, you've forgotten all your capital letters. Go back and fix that." Aaron would trot back to his desk, sit down, and after a bit of fooling around, get to work correcting the capital letters. In the end, his draft would be better, but he hadn't learning anything about improving his own work.

To help Aaron develop the ability to monitor his own progress, his teachers needed to ***ask him questions*** instead of telling him what to fix. In this scenario, when Aaron came to the teacher with the draft of his essay, she could have said something like this: "Aaron, I'm glad you got a draft done. Can you figure out what you need to do next?" If

Aaron didn't answer, she could scaffold his thinking by reminding him of resources in the classroom. "Aaron, where can you look to help you think about what to do next?" If there was still no answer, she could scaffold it a bit more. "Is there a chart on the wall that can help you?" The trick here is to avoid pointing out the chart to Aaron—the minute the teacher points it out to him, he stops thinking and starts depending on her guidance. The effective teacher will scaffold questions to Aaron until he can identify that there is a chart on the wall that tells him the steps of the writing process and that the next step is for him to edit his spelling. By asking questions and scaffolding his answers, the teacher teaches Aaron that he already has the answers—he just has to know where to look.

Obviously, this is a little more time consuming than just telling Aaron to go fix the capital letters, but in the end, it can change Aaron from a passive learner to an active one. The time you take up front to scaffold a student's ability to monitor his progress *independently* will save you hours down the line; you will no longer have to keep sending Aaron back to his seat to redo his work. He will be able to identify and complete the next steps on his own.

GUIDELINES #8 & #9:
PROVIDING OPTIONS FOR EXPRESSION & COMMUNICATION AND PHYSICAL ACTION

Throughout this book, we've examined the scenarios that occur when students with learning difficulties are not given opportunities to show what they know. This is one of the biggest challenges of inclusive classrooms and is a particular problem when we are talking about writing instruction. UDL asks us to give students different choices of ways to show they're learning, but with writing it's a bit tricky—you can't ask a student to make a video when the instructional objective is to see if she can express herself logically in writing . . . or can you? Are there ways that we can "open up" our expectations in regard to writing and still meet the requirements of the Common Core? In this section, we will explore that question, and we will consider some creative ways to allow your students to have options for expression.

Using Multiple Media

These days, there is a myriad of wonderful media our students can choose to help them communicate. As digital natives, it's second nature for many students to want to use a variety of media in their learning; being digital immigrants, we as teachers have to work to expand our thinking beyond paper and pencil to the contemporary world of video, online writing, social media, discussion forums, and many other possibilities (Prensky, 2001).

Indeed, there is a great big world of multimedia writing opportunities out there, and clearly this was on the minds of the developers of the Common Core when they wrote Standard Number 10: Writing for a range of discipline specific tasks, purposes, and audiences. Even when our students are working on the "conventional" standards of writing, i.e., narrative (W.3), informational (W.2), and argument (W.1), we can expand our ideas beyond pencil and paper (or keyboard and paper) to expressive media that will engage a wider range of learners and motivate them to write creatively.

Synthesizing Reading

In one of the university courses I teach, I ask my students to identify three big ideas from their readings each week and to represent those ideas in a creative fashion. They need to elaborate on them enough that I can tell they read and synthesized the information, but they need to do so in a way that stretches them to go beyond the traditional reading reflection that so many of us

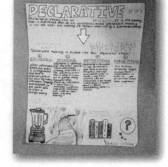

have written over the years. I do this for two reasons. First, this is the class in which they learn how to apply UDL, and I want them to experience first-hand some of the options they can use when they are teaching students in their own classrooms. Secondly, the creative reading reflections are much more enjoyable for me to grade than a traditional reading reflection! Do these creative reflections still require them to synthesize information and make meaning of it?

Absolutely! In fact, I would argue that they have to evaluate what they've read at a very high level in order to choose what they consider to be the three most important ideas and elaborate on them briefly.

These photographs show some examples of creative reading reflections that my students have done over the years. As you are teaching your students to research for their writing (W.7, W.8, W.9), think about creative options for them to organize and synthesize what they learn before

they begin to put words to paper. It will make your classroom a more exciting, engaging place and will motivate your learners to do the hard work of identifying what is really important from their research.

Using Comics and Other Visual Media

In Chapter 5, we looked at some fun tools for storyboarding, such as Bitstrips and StoryboardThat, and we discussed the importance of minimizing the amount of text when storyboarding in order to focus on the big ideas of the story. However, comics and other visual media such as videos and slide shows can be used to fulfill many of the requirements of the CCSS in creative and appealing ways. Figure 7.9 is an example of one page of a cartoon created using Comic Life (http://plasq.com), an interactive program that allows students to make incredible graphic stories on the computer. Let's examine this for its alignment to CCSS W.8.2, the eighth-grade standards for writing informational text.

Writing standard W.8.2.A mentions multimedia as a way to help students organize and format ideas. As you can see from this example, the format of the cartoon provides a wonderful scaffold for sequential organization of informational text.

Figure 7.9 Using Comic Life to Write Informational Text

Copyright © G. Bledsoe, 2006. Reproduced with permission.

At the eighth-grade level, students are also expected to develop a topic with well-chosen details and examples (W.8.2.B). The comic book format forces students to include only the most important details in their comics, both visually and in words.

Standard W.8.2.D asks students to use precise language in their informational writing. In this example, the student used rich, specific vocabulary in his descriptions, and the pictures support the reader in making meaning of the vocabulary.

Figure 7.10 presents another example of Comic Life. In this one, a student (or in this case a dog) is interviewing poet Liz Brownlee about her writing process. It's easy to tell from this example how this tool would increase the motivation and engagement of reluctant writers, as well as provide a visual tool for them to organize their thoughts and expand on their ideas. More information about Liz Brownlee and her poems for children can be found at www.poetlizbrownlee.co.uk.

Want to see more examples of Comic Life in the classroom? Check out the Comic Life Twitter page, at twitter.com/ComicLife. The ReadWriteThink website also offers an interesting lesson in using Comic Life to help students identify stereotypical thinking in characters at www.readwritethink.org/ classroom-resources/lesson-plans/comic-makeovers-examining-race-207 .html. If you're truly adventurous, explore Motion Artist at motionartist. smithmicro.com. This application lets you take comic writing to a whole new level, creating comics that move, with 3-D, backgrounds, and overlapping images. Thank you to middle school teacher Glen Bledsoe for his beautiful Comic Life example above and for introducing me to Motion Artist. You can see more of his work at www.crazyflycomics.com.

Digital Storytelling

There are lots of student-made videos available on the Web, some of which are strong examples of the application of higher-level writing skills to a different medium. Check out the zombie video made by fifth-grade students in Bethke Elementary School in Timnath, Colorado: www .youtube.com/watch?v=uHOOOG5cMVM. This video has some wonderful exemplars of the fifth-grade Common Core writing standards. For instance, they organized their events logically and created a strong narrator voice (W.5.3.A), used a variety of narrative techniques to develop the experience (W.5.3.B), used a range of transitions and transition words in the narrative (W.5.3.C), and used the character's dialogue to create sensory details that produce a strong sense of suspense and story (W.5.3.D).

Figure 7.10   Using Comic Life to "Interview" a Poet

Video can be a powerful tool for both narrative and expository writing, and most of the requirements of the Common Core can be practiced in this medium. It is, by nature, very motivating to this generation of children who were raised on video communication. Additionally, it is a medium in which there will only be more employment opportunities in the future!

Tools for Physical Access and Composition

Another important consideration in the UDL classroom is physical access—some students can't truly participate without some special tools to help them access the curriculum. This includes assistive tools for physical access such as alternative keyboards, as well as expressive tools for composition such as speech to text. The purpose of both types of tools is to give students the ability to actually express what is in their heads. In the words of CAST, the tendency of schools to use traditional tools "constricts the kinds of learners who can be successful." Equally important, our students need to have the option to use a variety of writing tools in order to learn which ones help them perform writing tasks successfully.

We have discussed many expressive tools in earlier chapters and explored their motivational power for struggling writers. Tools such as speech to text, spell and grammar check, and word prediction software provide students with language-based disabilities the opportunity to overcome their limitations and express themselves. Table 7.1 provides a few more apps and programs that we haven't discussed; I hope these will be powerful additions to your toolbox.

Tables 7.2 and 7.3 give a great overview of some of the accessibility features that can help students participate in general education activities with parity.

For many of us, it's hard to let go of the idea that writing skills always need to be practiced by taking pen to paper to write a story, composition, or essay. Many teachers today went to school in a time when that was the only option. However, the modern world now dictates that much of the writing that our students will do in the workplace will be in other formats and media; in fact, the top ten in-demand jobs in 2010 didn't even exist in 2004, so there is a good chance that we are preparing our students to do jobs that we can't even imagine. Given these startling facts, it behooves us to offer our students a wide range of experiences beyond the old-fashioned essays students have been writing for hundreds of years. Push yourself to expand your teaching to include more of these interactive and engaging writing options. It will benefit all your students and will make your classroom a lot more fun for everyone—including you!

Table 7.1 Expressive Writing Tools

Tool	Purpose
Keyboard Commands	For students with fine- or gross-motor limitations, using the mouse can sometimes be difficult. Keyboard shortcuts allow students to complete many of the same functions as the mouse but using the keyboard instead of the mouse. Shortcuts are specific to the device, and in many cases, you can make your own to suit your needs.
Clicker	The Clicker language arts programs can be purchased as software for the computer or apps for the iPad. There are activities to support sentence building, reading comprehension, and writing, designed to be used by students with a range of abilities. http://www.cricksoft.com/us/home.aspx
Co:Writer for iPad	This classic word-prediction software by Don Johnston (one of the first on the market) now has an app that can be used on the iPad and iPhone to make writing more accessible for all students. The app is very intuitive and easy to use, and most children will learn it easily. http://donjohnston.com/cowriterapp/#.U_DxToBdWlQ
Draft: Builder	Another piece of software by Don Johnston, Draft: Builder gives students one tool that helps them outline in graphic-organizer format, elaborate on the outline with notes, and build a draft from their notes. http://donjohnston.com/draftbuilder/#.U_DwvYBdWlQ
CAST Strategy Tutor	Strategy Tutor is an online tool designed to scaffold students through the process of doing research on the Web. Virtual coaches help students evaluate the quality of websites, guide students to think about comprehension strategies as they work, and help them keep track of their work. http://cast.org/learningtools/strategy_tutor/index.html
Research Project Calculator	The RPC provides step-by-step guidelines for students as they work through different types of assignments. The writing assignment guidelines walk them through the process of gathering information, organizing and evaluating that information, and writing their essay. https://rpc.elm4you.org

Table 7.2 Accessibility Tools for iPad, Mac, and iPhone (iOS)

Feature	Touch Screen	Mac
VoiceOver	iOS systems include VoiceOver, a screen reader for the devices and apps. It voices text on the home page, in apps, and in web browsers. In the Camera app, VoiceOver will tell you how many people are in your shot and where they are on the screen. In Photos, VoiceOver will tell you the date of a photo, its orientation, whether it's crisp or blurry, and how well lit it is.	Turn on VoiceOver for Mac by going to System Preferences > Accessibility > Enable VoiceOver. It will provide vocal descriptions of menu items and voice control of the keyboard.
Speak Selection	Highlight text in almost any application, tap Speak, and the selected text will be read aloud. Dialect and speaking rate can be adjusted and words can be highlighted as they're being read. Speak Selection doesn't work in the Kindle app, so it can't be used for reading Kindle books out loud.	Some (but not all) web browsers have speak-text options. In Chrome and Safari, highlight text, then choose Edit > Speech > Start speaking.
Voice Commands	Hold down the Home key and Siri will ask you for voice commands that can be used to turn on accessibility features, send messages, search the Internet, etc.	Speakable Items will allow you to control your computer and applications through voice commands. System Preferences > Accessibility > Speakable Items
Dictation	Tap the microphone button on the keyboard and dictate your words. The iOS device converts your words, numbers, and characters into text.	In Microsoft Word, choose Edit, start dictation, or tap the function key twice.
Dictionary	Tap a word using two fingers, and then chose "Look Up in Dictionary" from the shortcut menu, or tap a word using three fingers.	In a document or webpage, you can get a definition by pressing the control key and clicking on a word, then choosing Look Up. Or select a word and press Command (⌘)-Option-Shift-R.

(Continued)

Table 7.2 (Continued)

Feature	Touch Screen	Mac
Zoom	A built-in magnifier that works whenever you are in iOS. Double-tapping with three fingers instantly zooms in 200 percent, and you can adjust the magnification between 100 and 500 percent. Settings > General > Accessibility > turn on Zoom	A built-in magnifier that works whenever you are in iOS. System Preferences > Accessibility > Zoom, will take you to the keyboard shortcuts.
Font Adjustments	The text systemwide can be converted to a larger size or made bold. Settings > General > Accessibility > turn on Larger Text and/or Bold Text	
Invert Colors	Inverts the onscreen colors systemwide. Settings > General > Accessibility > turn on Invert Colors	Inverts the onscreen colors systemwide. System Preferences > Accessibility > Display > turn on Invert Colors or Use grayscale.
Background Contrast	Increase the contrast on some backgrounds to improve legibility. Settings > General > Accessibility > turn on Increase Contrast	Increase the contrast on some backgrounds to improve legibility. System Preferences > Accessibility > Display > slide Enhance Contrast. You can also change the size of the cursor from the same site.
Guided Access	Can restrict iPad to a single app temporarily by disabling the home button and restricting touch input to certain areas of the screen. Settings > General > Accessibility along with instructions on how to use it	
Personalized Keyboard Shortcuts	A keyboard shortcut can easily be created for common words or phrases. Settings > General > Keyboard > Add New Shortcut	A keyboard shortcut can easily be created for common words, phrases or commands. Settings > General > Keyboard
Turn on Accessibility Feature From Home Button	Settings > General > Accessibility > Accessibility Shortcut to select features you use the most	

Feature	Touch Screen	Mac
Mono Audio	Plays both audio channels in both ears instead of in stereo (distinct left and right audio tracks).	
Visible and Vibrating Alerts	For e-mail, text messages, calendar, phone, and FaceTime, an LED light flash or vibration patterns can be set.	
Custom Gestures	Gestures like rotate and shake are available to replace pinch or other gestures difficult or impossible for an individual. AssistiveTouch is located in Settings > General > Accessibility.	
Home-Click Speed	Change the speed required to activate double- and triple-click home commands. Just go to Settings > General > Accessibility > Home-Click Speed.	Change the speed of your mouse or trackpad by going to System Preferences > Mouse (or trackpad).
Closed Captions	Look for the CC icon for captions and subtitles. You can even customize captions with different styles and fonts. Settings > General > Accessibility > tap Subtitles & Captioning	You can customize captions with different styles and fonts. System Preferences > Accessibility > Captions
Braille	Over forty Bluetooth wireless braille displays are supported by later iOS devices. Once paired, it can be used to navigate an iOS device with VoiceOver. iPad, iPhone, and iPod Touch include braille tables for more than twenty-five languages.	
Switch Control	Can navigate through onscreen items and perform specific actions using a variety of Bluetooth-enabled switch hardware. Control your iPad, iPhone, or iPod Touch using head movements and your device's camera. You'll find Switch Control in Settings > General > Accessibility.	Can navigate through onscreen items and perform specific actions using a variety of Bluetooth-enabled switch hardware. System Preferences > Accessibility > Switch Control

Table 7.3 Accessibility Tools for Windows 7 and 8

Feature	Description
Ease of Access Center	Provides a centralized location where you can adjust accessibility settings and programs. You can also get recommendations for settings to make your PC easier to see, hear, and use.
Magnifier	Magnifies the screen or a portion of the screen to make text, images, and objects easier to see.
On-Screen Keyboard	A visual, on-screen keyboard with all the standard keys that you can use instead of a physical keyboard. On-Screen Keyboard also lets you type and enter data with a mouse or other pointing device.
Narrator	Reads aloud on-screen text and describes some events that occur or error messages that appear while you're using the computer.
Speech Recognition	Enables you to interact with your computer using only your voice while maintaining, or even increasing, your productivity.
Change Text Size	Lets you make text and objects larger and easier to see without losing graphics quality.
Personalization	You can add a personal touch to your computer by changing the computer's theme, color, sounds, desktop background, screen saver, font size, and more.
Touch	If you've got a touch-screen monitor, you can just touch your computer screen for a more direct and natural way to work. Use your fingers to scroll, resize windows, play media, and pan and zoom.
Keyboard Shortcuts	Keyboard combinations of two or more keys that, when pressed, can be used to perform a task that would typically require a mouse or other pointing device. Keyboard shortcuts can make it easier to interact with your computer, saving you time and effort.
Sticky Keys	Instead of having to press three keys at once (such as when you must press the Ctrl, Alt, and Delete keys simultaneously to log on to Windows), you can press one key at a time when Sticky Keys is turned on.
Mouse Keys	Instead of using the mouse, you can use the arrow keys on the numeric keypad to move the pointer.
Filter Keys	Ignore keystrokes that occur in rapid succession and keystrokes that are held down for several seconds unintentionally.
Visual Notifications	Replace system sounds with visual cues, such as a flash on the screen, so system alerts are announced with visual notifications instead of sounds.

Table 7.4 Accessible Apps for Students Who Need More Support in Expression

Application	Description	Cost
Story Wheel	Story Wheel is an app for the iPad and iPhone targeting cognitive abilities. It is a game designed to promote storytelling. Players record a story by spinning the wheel to get a picture and then narrate a story.	Free or $2.99 for more thematic sets of images
Book Creator	Create iBooks on iPad.	$4.99
Little Bird Tales	A storytelling and e-learning tool designed to create digital stories. Multimedia stories can be created with images, text, and/or narrated.	Web based
Animation Desk	An iPad app for creating short animated videos. Create scenes from drawings using your finger on the screen. Different brush and pencil effects and colors can be customized.	Free
Alexicom Elements Story Maker	Story templates with text-to-speech and recorded audio options, word prediction with a 150,000-word library, and switch support.	$9.99
Pictello	Create multimedia stories and presentations using pictures from the iPad photo library. Audio can be produced using a text-to-speech engine or can be recorded.	$18.99
Clicker Docs	A writing tool that provides differentiated support for individuals of all abilities through word prediction and spelling and grammatical suggestions. Word banks can also be created.	$30.99
Clicker Sentences	An early writing tool that supports sentence building.	$28.99

WRAPPING UP THE BIG IDEAS

- Executive-function skills help us plan, organize, and manage our work and our lives. They can be problematic for many students and need to be taught and supported in the classroom.
- Teachers need to break writing tasks down into discrete steps to help students set short- and long-term goals in writing.

(Continued)

(Continued)

- In order to reduce the demands on working memory, let students use technology and peer support to focus on one thing at a time during the writing process.
- Use questioning to scaffold students' independence in the classroom; don't tell them—ask them!
- Allow students to practice writing skills in other media such as video, comics, and creative projects.
- Use assistive tools to help students meet the expressive and physical demands of writing.

FOR FURTHER READING

Ellis, E. S., Deshler, D. D., Lenz, B., Schumaker, J. B., & Clark, F. L. (1991). An instructional model for teaching learning strategies. *Focus on Exceptional Children, 23*(6), 1–23.

National Center for Learning Disabilities. (n.d.). What is executive function? Retrieved from http://www.ncld.org/types-learning-disabilities/executive-function-disorders/what-is-executive-function

Schumaker, J. B., & Deshler, D. D. (2009). Adolescents with learning disabilities as writers: Are we selling them short? *Learning Disabilities Research and Practice, 24*(2), 81–92.

Closing Thoughts **8**

Identify your assets.
Celebrate your strengths.
Plan your progress.
YOU HAVE WHAT IT
TAKES.

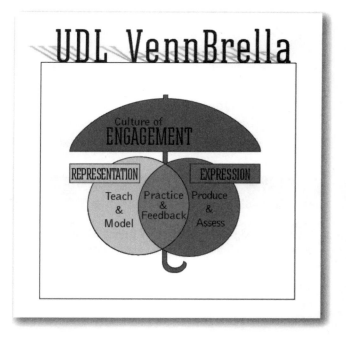

The statements above are a perfect snapshot of what UDL asks us to do—identify and celebrate our students' strengths, then use that knowledge to help them plan their way forward. This strategy obviously applies to our students, but it also applies beautifully to teachers. Teachers need to identify their *own* strengths and assets as education professionals before they can begin the process of creating a classroom that is universally designed and accessible for all students.

This final chapter has two purposes—first, to help you take some essential first steps toward universally designed writing instruction in your classroom. In this chapter, you will have the opportunity to explore the assets of your class, identify the gaps, and prepare a plan to more fully implement UDL in your class.

Second, there are some frequently asked questions that often come up when we are discussing UDL, and I would like to use this chapter to address some of the questions that may remain.

CREATING THE UNIVERSALLY DESIGNED WRITING CLASSROOM

Identify Your Assets

In order to create a universally designed writing classroom, first you need to identify what you are already doing well. As you've read through this book, no doubt you have stopped to pat yourself on the back along the way, acknowledging the many strong instructional practices that you already have in place. It's possible that you are already implementing most of the big ideas in this book and can proudly proclaim your writing instruction to be universally designed. If you still have a ways to go, though, then the first step is to identify your strengths and highlight the gaps that you could improve. Table 8.1 provides a starting place for this work—this thirty-item checklist is created from the big ideas in the book and will serve as a jumping-off point for your work.

Table 8.1 Checklist for Identifying Teacher Strengths and Assets

I have a good understanding of the elements of writing that make it difficult for my struggling students, especially those with disabilities (Ch. 1).
I have identified which of the elements (Ch. 1) my struggling writers have strengths in, and which they are having difficulty with.
I am clear about what I value in terms of writing, and how it affects my writing instruction.
I have a strong understanding of the four big ideas of the Common Core writing standards (Ch. 2) and how they interact with one another.
I have a strong understanding of the three types of writing emphasized in the CCSS (Ch. 2) and how they differ from one another.
I have familiarized myself with the six elements of the Common Core language standards (Ch. 2), and I understand how they interact with the writing standards to create strong writers.
I believe that the diversity in my classroom is natural, and that I can teach all kids.
I understand the three elements of UDL, and what they look like in classroom practice (Ch. 3).
I understand the importance of separating the goal from the means so that I can provide students with options that allow them to access the goal (Ch. 3).
I teach my students about the hidden curriculum in writing (Ch. 4).

I understand how to use technology to help my students develop independence in their writing and to avoid learned helplessness (Ch. 4 & 7).
I use specific, mastery-oriented feedback that helps my students understand and appreciate their own growth (Ch. 4).
I provide my students choices to motivate and empower them (Ch. 4) including • where and when to complete writing tasks, • what types of tools and instruments they can use to write, • levels of challenge of different assignments, • topics to write about, and • reinforcers, including how work is published.
I explicitly teach and model the use of mnemonic devices and graphic organizers for writing and provide my students with opportunities to memorize and practice the tools (Ch. 5).
I teach my students to use a variety of organizers and tools and help them learn how to choose the appropriate one for each writing task (Ch. 5).
I have my students analyze and compare different types of writing across purposes and genres (Ch. 5).
I help my students break down and discuss student work samples, using the language of our graphic organizers (Ch. 5).
I give my struggling writers the opportunity to analyze and discuss writing samples in small groups.
I teach my struggling writers Latin and Greek roots and how to generalize their meanings to new words to increase students' vocabulary (Ch. 6).
I teach my students how to use context clues to interpret new vocabulary and to understand how synonyms are similar and different from one another (Ch. 6).
I use visual supports to help my students understand synonyms, antonyms, figurative language, and new vocabulary (Ch. 6).
I provide my students with strategies to help them apply new vocabulary to their writing (Ch. 6).
I help my struggling writers learn to create good, clear, simple sentences first, then teach them how to create more complex sentences (Ch. 6).
I teach my students to use web-based tools that can help them access text when they are researching (Ch. 6).
I break writing tasks down into small steps and use checklists to help my students understand the processes (Ch. 7).
I help my students set long- and short-term goals for their writing (Ch. 7).
I teach my students to do multiple passes during revision and editing to reduce demands on working memory (Ch. 7).
I build students' executive functioning by asking questions to scaffold their independence rather than telling them what to do (Ch. 7).
I give my students creative options to express their learning rather than the same kinds of essays over and over (Ch. 7).
I allow students to practice writing in other media such as videos and comics (Ch. 7).

Get More Information

I've no doubt that you have identified many practices in the list above that you have already integrated into your regular classroom routines. However, if you're like me, there might be some areas in which you could still use some work. The next step is to decide how to go about filling any gaps you identified. Table 8.2 provides some areas in which you might consider getting more information and some resources you can explore to do so. If you feel like you don't need more information or you can get enough information by going back to the chapters, then move on to the next step, "Documenting Your Resources."

Document Potential Resources

If you've found some areas that you would like to improve, the next step is to investigate and document your resources. For this, you need to think outside the box a bit; you may not have those iPads you covet, but your students may have smartphones that will do a lot of the same work! I like to think of it in terms of the following categories:

Expertise/Support. Who do you have available to help you with this process? Is there another teacher at your school who knows a lot about teaching writing or UDL? Do you have a former college professor you can e-mail? Reach out to the folks that have the expertise and enlist their support. Just knowing you have someone else who is on your side, cheering you on, can make a huge difference. Arrange a bimonthly happy hour with that person to discuss your progress and get guidance.

Technology. Although you don't *have* to use technology to implement universally designed writing instruction, it can be really helpful as a support for many students. Think broadly about this—do you or your students have iPods, iPads, smartphones, tape recorders, old computers, Elmos . . . ? Any of those tools can be a huge benefit. Also, take a good look around your school. I was in a middle school a year or so ago and found thirty-five old laptops stuck in a cupboard. They weren't much good for accessing the Internet, but they were great for word processing, and no one even knew they were there anymore! I can't tell you how many

Table 8.2   Where to Get More Information

Area of Need	Resources
Understanding the writing challenges of students with disabilities	National Center for Learning Disabilities: http://www.ncld.org LD Online: http://www.ldonline.org/article/What_Is_Dysgraphia%3F International Dyslexia Association: http://eida.org/understanding-dysgraphia/
Understanding the Common Core Writing Standards	Achieve the Core: http://achievethecore.org/page/507/in-common-effective-writing-for-all-students *Pathways to the Common Core: Accelerating Achievement* by Lucy Calkins, Mary Ehrenworth, Christopher Lehman (2012)
Universal Design for Learning	National Center on UDL: http://www.udlcenter.org *Universal Design for Learning: Theory and Practice* by Meyer, Rose, and Gordon (2014) Available free on line at http://udltheorypractice.cast.org/login
Using technology to support struggling writers	Understood: https://www.understood.org/en/about/search-results?q=dysgraphia Paths to Literacy: http://www.pathstoliteracy.org/technology-students-multiple-disabilities LD Online: http://www.ldonline.org/article/6397 Adolescent Literacy.org: http://www.adlit.org/article/35792
Explicit teaching of learning strategies	National Center on Learning Disabilities: http://www.ncld.org/students-disabilities/ld-education-teachers/strategic-instruction-model-how-teach-how-learn The IRIS Center: http://iris.peabody.vanderbilt.edu/iris-resource-locator Teaching LD.org: http://s3.amazonaws.com/cmi-teaching-ld/alerts/3/uploaded_files/original_alert17writingSSRD.pdf?1301000388
Teaching vocabulary and language	*Powerful Writing Strategies for All Students* by Karen Harris, Steve Graham, Linda Mason, Barbara Friedlander *Bringing Word to Life (2nd ed.)* by Isabel Beck, Margaret McKeown, and Linda Kucan (2013) Edutopia: http://www.edutopia.org/blog/vocabulary-instruction-teaching-tips-rebecca-alber LD Online: http://www.ldonline.org/article/The_Clarifying_Routine%3A_Elaborating_Vocabulary_Instruction Reading Rockets: http://www.readingrockets.org/article/best-practice-ells-vocabulary-instruction

schools have SmartBoards stuck in closets because the teachers don't know how to use them.

Time. Obviously time is a factor in anything new you try. I always tell new teachers to try to create one fantastic lesson a week during their first year of teaching. The same principle applies here. ***Try to find the time to implement one new support or tool a week.*** Maybe it will be that you will teach the students how to use speech to text, or maybe it will be that you will use multiple ways of representing your content. But every tiny step you make takes you closer to UDL! The important thing is this: *don't try to do everything at once!* Take your time and take small steps toward your goal. Then pat yourself on the back for making positive changes in your classroom.

Materials. What books, graphic organizers, charts, posters, and so on do you have? What more do you need? Do you have some interesting writing utensils that students can use? How about colored paper? Are there some study carrels stuck away in a closet somewhere that you can use to make "offices"? Make a list of what you wish you had and give it to an administrator—materials are one of the places that they are often willing to spend a little money. Also, consider using Donor's Choose to fill in some of the gaps—it's a powerful resource for many teachers (www.donorschoose .org), and I know many teachers who have gotten Elmos, iPads, and other great equipment through Donor's Choose.

Create a Plan

As we talk about creating a plan, I want to refer you back to the paragraph above on time. Anyone who has ever been a teacher knows that you have *tons* on your plate and that you need to be careful not to overcommit yourself when you try something new. Your time is your most precious and scarce resource. So as I mentioned before, don't try to do this all at once. Identify a few things you can change at a time, and take baby steps to your ultimate goal. Below are some steps you can follow to help you identify what you can change easily and perhaps some items you want to work on over time.

Write a Long-Term Goal

What do you hope to accomplish during this school year? Be specific in your wording—what *specific* elements of UDL would you like to see going strong in your classroom by the end of the year?

_____

_____

Identify the Easy Stuff

Are there changes you can make easily? Below is a checklist of some small changes that you might be able to make without too much effort—check off the ones that will work for you. Remember, this is *your* plan. Just because I've identified them as potentially "easy" doesn't mean they will be for you.

Notes:

☐ Create writing objectives that separate the goal from the means and give students options for expression.

☐ Do some lessons on the hidden curriculum in writing.

☐ Stockpile some interesting paper choices and writing instruments.

☐ Explicitly teach the use of graphic organizers, with opportunities to memorize and practice.

☐ Gather a bank of graphic organizers that can be used for different types of writing.

☐ Help student break writing down into discrete steps and use checklists to guide them.

☐ Teach students to make multiple passes during editing.

_____
_____
_____
_____
_____
_____
_____
_____
_____
_____
_____
_____
_____
_____
_____
_____
_____

Write a short-term goal. What makes sense to do next? Go back to Table 8.1 (or somewhere else in the book) and choose one thing that isn't quite so easy that you would like to tackle next. Again, consider your time, your students, and your instructional needs. Also think about the supports and tools you have before you make this decision.

My next steps are: _____

_____

Who will help me? _____

_____

*What tools/equipment/materials do I need to take these steps?*____

If you keep your short-term goals clear, simple, and achievable, and carefully consider your time and resources before you make them, before you know it, it'll be June, and you will have made significant steps toward your universally designed classroom. However, in case questions remain, the last section in this chapter is designed to answer some of the frequently asked questions that come up as teachers, schools, and school districts begin to consider the implementation of UDL. I hope they will answer yours as well.

FREQUENTLY ASKED QUESTIONS

FAQ #1: Can UDL Be Implemented Without Technology?

 Since the foundations of UDL came out of assistive and instructional technology, many people wonder if they can implement UDL in their classrooms without it. This is a question that even the founders of CAST have asked themselves, and they have provided a link on their website to a sample lesson that tests that theory: http://www.udlcenter.org/sites/udlcenter.org/files/notech_final2.pdf.

What they found is that, yes, the instructional concepts embedded in UDL can be followed, even in a classroom that has little or no access to technology. Teachers can make lessons that provide students with options for expression and engagement and which support individuality and choice. They can support executive functioning through structures that guide students to work independently, and they can provide tools that allow students with limited mobility to function alongside their typically developing peers (Edyburn, 2005).

Can we create UDL *writing* lessons without technology? Absolutely, but you will have to think of ways to provide options that support students with difficulties in the various areas discussed in Chapter 1. Instead of giving students the option to dictate text into an electronic device, for example, you can let them choose to work with a partner who can function as a scribe. This option will support students with a wide array of physical and cognitive needs and provides a nice alternative for all the students to try something different. Personal dictionaries and word walls can be helpful to all students but especially for those with memory deficits or language delays who don't have access to technology. Your students will appreciate the opportunity to try out different types of pencil grips, writing instruments, and papers, and for those with fine-motor deficits, these options can make the writing process much more fluid.

There are lots of nontechnological options discussed throughout this book, but realistically, if you can get your hands on some technology, the design of your UDL writing classroom will be much easier. As mentioned above, think broadly about the technology available to you and your students. You may find out that you have lots of tools that you hadn't considered using before, such as students' personal cell phones or those laptops from the old computer lab; and remember, you don't need everyone to have the same tools at the same time. What you want is options, so that all the students have the opportunity to try out a variety of technologies and see what works best for them.

FAQ #2: What About Accommodations and Modifications?

Even people who are well informed about UDL are sometimes confused about how UDL fits into the bigger picture of adapting work to meet the individual needs of students. One of the biggest differences between UDL and the older paradigm of adapting work is that UDL is *proactive.* Universally designed lessons create a range of accessible options from the very beginning and build those options into the curriculum so that all students can experience them. This naturally reduces the stigma attached to being the child who is doing "something different" in the classroom, but almost as important, it is actually *easier for the teachers.* In UDL, teachers develop the habit of considering the range of learners in their classroom as normal and put away the old-fashioned idea that there are a group of "normal" students in the middle and outliers around the edges who need something different. Because teachers using UDL consider the spectrum of learners from the start, they no longer have to go back to their lessons after they are designed and create a boatload of individually adapted materials for each of the five to ten students in their classes who have special learning, language, or physical needs.

Does this mean you will never have to adapt curriculum again? Admittedly, no. There will always be students whose needs are so unique that they will need some special tools that other students won't. For example, if you have a student who is blind, he or she may require braille text, which would be of no use to your other students. On the other hand, if that student uses a screen reader or some other text-to-speech device, it may be something that can benefit a wide variety of students in your classroom, and it may become part of your everyday UDL toolbox. Other tools, such as special joystick, switches, keyboards, or adaptors, may be too complex or expensive to offer to every child and will only be available for those students whose needs dictate their use.

In a classroom where diversity is recognized as the norm, reducing barriers for those students who have the most significant needs is a natural function, and the founders of CAST recognize assistive technology as a partner to UDL. They picture both pieces as part of a continuum of accessibility, with an overlapping boundary that merges the two pieces together into a seamless whole (Rose, Hasselbring, Stahl, & Zabala, 2005). If you have a student in your class who has such significant needs that he or she needs special assistive technology, consider that as an addendum to your UDL, but don't stop thinking about other instructional options that give the student access to the curriculum in conjunction with the assistive tools.

One of the benefits of UDL is that it can reduce the inequity that often comes along with adaptations—for example, delays while adaptations are being implemented or the necessity for a different location or special assistance in order to access the curriculum. Our goal is to create a classroom where the curriculum becomes accessible for all children with as few inequities as possible. While there will always be some students who might need something extra, UDL helps us to reduce the barriers to accessibility on a classwide level before we provide individual accommodations for students who need them. That reduces the stigma and bias for all the students and the workload for the educators—a win-win situation!

FAQ #3: Will UDL Work for Students With More Significant Cognitive and Physical Needs?

Throughout the book, you have read about ways to make learning more accessible for students of all abilities. Since the vast majority of students identified with special needs fall within the mild-to-moderate range (such as learning disabilities, students with ADHD, and many students on the autism spectrum), we have focused much of our attention on them. In the previous FAQ, we discussed some special accessibility devices that might be needed by students with more significant needs, and it is clear that some students will still need special devices, such as switches, keyboards, communication devices, and so on, in order to access the curriculum. But that doesn't mean that UDL doesn't work for those students. Even for students with the most significant needs, it is still important to consider your instructional goals in the broadest sense to make them applicable to all students and to allow all students to show what they know. Here we will examine some general principles related to making writing instruction accessible to students with more significant needs and, more specifically, look at how those needs can intersect with the Common Core standards in writing.

Writing Instruction for Students With Significant Disabilities

Just as with any other student, you cannot generalize about teaching writing to students with significant learning and physical needs. The needs of this population are specific to the students and vary widely. For some students, there may be parts of the Common Core writing standards that you can pull out and use as guidelines for instruction, whereas for others, your objectives will be much narrower, such as writing their names at the top of their paper. Nevertheless, there are some strategies you can use to help make your writing instruction more meaningful if you have a student with a significant disability in your classroom. The following principles are summarized from the CAST website and other research, as well as from the book *Teaching Literacy to Students with Significant Disabilities: Strategies for the K–12 Inclusive Classroom*, by my wonderful, departed colleague June Downing (2005). The resources at the end of this chapter should be of help to you if you need more information about successfully teaching writing to this population.

What Is Literacy?

In order to successfully include students with more significant needs in our writing instruction, we need to broaden our definition of literacy to include alternative forms of expression. Writing may include writing with pictures, telling a story by sequencing objects, using magnetic letters or words to communicate a sequence of events, or using software programs such as Clicker (www.cricksoft.com/us) or First Author (donjohnston.com/firstauthorsoftware). We also need to take into account the nature of writing as a function of communication. For students with significant disabilities, their primary method of communication may be an augmentative communication device, and the process of selecting and appropriately using the device is akin to writing. Students who have limitations on physical movement, speech, cognition, or all of these may use a communication device to tell a simple story, such as "I like Mathew," and their writing objectives may be formulated around that type of communicative interaction.

Learning Objectives

As I've mentioned before, it's important to state your learning objectives broadly, with a focus on the true purpose of the learning, so that students can enter them at a developmental level that is appropriate for each student. Instead of saying, "Students will write an essay about . . . " you might say something like, "Students will demonstrate their understanding of . . . " That allows for a broader range of responses that can allow your students with more significant needs to participate in the same learning objective as the rest of the class. If you are not stating your goals in this way, you may be inadvertently limiting the ways students can show what they learned. For some students, prerequisite skills to essay writing, such as identifying characters, choosing a setting, and identifying a big idea will be appropriate learning goals that will allow them to participate alongside their typical peers.

Making It Meaningful

As we've discussed in previous chapters, all students need to have learning that is meaningful to them, and for students with more significant learning needs, the Language Experience approach can be a powerful tool that connects them to writing by asking them to tell about an experience in their lives. Students can be asked to sequence a series of photographs that tell about a field trip or birthday party or choose the appropriate items on a communication board to tell the story. Other options would allow them to verbally sequence ideas (that can be transcribed by someone else) or to use a Cloze format to fill in missing words, such as, "Yesterday we went on a field trip to _____." Obviously these options can be adjusted for the individual needs of any given student, and many of them, such as allowing students to use pictures to plan their writing, can be helpful to the whole class. Providing the option to write about a topic that is very concrete, familiar, and meaningful is particularly important for this population of students, and many students will engage in writing instruction when communicating about a topic they care about.

Incorporating Choice

As we have seen, the idea of choice or options is one of the most powerful and fundamental pieces of UDL. Research with students with significant learning needs has shown that this can be a valuable tool for them as well. Allowing them to choose the topic they write about or the order in which they complete classroom tasks has been shown to decrease off-task classroom behaviors in students of all different types of learning profiles.

Teaming With the Family

One of the most critical pieces to creating a meaningful educational experience for a student with a significant disability is to communicate with the family. This is important for all kids but particularly so for students whose learning strengths may not be readily apparent at a casual glance. Families of children with significant disabilities have information that they can share about what the students understand, what they can communicate, and what they care about. All of this could take months for a classroom teacher to discover without the expert input from the family. Additionally, the family needs input on what their hopes are for their child's literacy growth. Perhaps they really want their child to be able to sign his or her name on a document. Perhaps they know that their child can retell events, and they can tell you what tools to use to let the child practice and hone that important literacy skill. It is not always easy to understand what a child with limited verbal and/or physical skills can do, and the family is the source for that critical information. A partnership with them can be a teacher's most valuable strategy!

Using the Common Core Writing
Standards With Students With Significant Disabilities

As I stated above, students with significant disabilities, just like all other kids, have a range of strengths and needs. The ways you connect their learning to the CCSS is going to depend on their levels of functioning, their facility with a variety of expressive tools, and their understanding of the concepts being discussed. Nevertheless, the Common Core writing standards can often serve as the framework within which you choose their activities, and UDL can serve as the means for them to participate as functioning members of the classroom.

Below are some Common Core writing standards, from which I've pulled out some skills that might be appropriate for a student with a more significant challenge. Use these examples to spur your imagination about how you can use UDL and the CCSS to successfully make your students with significant disabilities members of your classroom community.

W.2.1. Write opinion pieces in which they introduce the topic or book they are writing about, state an opinion, supply reasons that support the opinion, use linking words (e.g., because, and, also) to connect opinion and reasons, and provide a concluding statement or section.

> *The students can state their opinions about the book using a Cloze format and communication board or other tool to "write" the opinions, e.g., "Wilbur (in* Charlotte's Web*) is a _____ pig." More advanced students can add a reason.*

W.4.2.B. Develop the topic with facts, definitions, concrete details, quotations, or other information and examples related to the topic.

> *The students can use Author's Choice to write one or two details about a topic, such as mammals. The program gives them pictures and words to choose from to create their sentences. A student with very significant physical and cognitive limitations might choose from three or four objects that relate to that topic, such as some fur, a small toy elephant, etc., and put them in order to communicate details about that topic.*

W.6.3.B. Use narrative techniques, such as dialogue, pacing, and description, to develop experiences, events, and/or characters.

> *The student might create a simple line of dialogue for a character by verbally telling it to someone or using a communication board. Some students might add relevant words into a prewritten sentence or might point to a word that a character might say.*

I want to encourage you to, as much as possible, use the same standards you are using for your whole class, focusing the participation a bit more narrowly where a student's needs demand it. That will help your students with the most significant needs become functioning parts of your UDL writing community.

TEACHER'S TALES

> *Many teachers, including myself when I was first in the classroom, question the value of this kind of literacy activity for students with very significant cognitive disabilities. "How can they benefit from this?" I wondered. "And wouldn't it be better just to teach them life skills such as using utensils, counting things, or tying their shoes?" Over the years, however, personal experience with students with a wide range of*

abilities has shown me that opportunities to be involved with literacy activities alongside typical peers can provide an array of benefits that we are only beginning to understand in the long term. I remember Ashley, who I met when she transferred from a school where it was believed that she was incapable of learning academic skills. Over time, Ashley learned to read and understand text at the fourth-grade level and blossomed into a beautiful young woman who went to prom and got a job. Did the literacy activities lead directly to this outcome? It can't be determined. But what I can tell you is that her interactions with her literacy teachers were one of the highlights of her academic life, and that I saw her learn and understand things that I didn't imagine possible when I first met her. I also think of Audrey, whose mother begged me to let her come to my literacy clinic because "she wasn't getting any academic skills in her high school classroom." Finally, I think of Joseph, a highly gifted young man whose strong sense of empathy and understanding has developed from his relationships with students with all types of abilities and skills in his inclusive classroom. These experiences and more have convinced me that welcoming students of all levels into our classrooms is appropriate, fair, and beneficial for everyone concerned and that UDL is the framework that makes this type of inclusive classroom an attainable proposition for teachers and schools.

THE FUTURE IS IN THE MARGINS

Let's face it: Change is hard. Creating classrooms that are different from those we grew up in asks us to step into the unknown and try things that may not be comfortable at first. UDL takes a new and different perspective on learning, learners, and the diverse nature of schools, going so far as to expect us to embrace a new understanding of "normal" (Meyer & Rose, 2005). None of this is easy, and none of this can happen without dedication, hard work, and an open mind.

Having said that, I want to remind you that every journey starts with one single step. And to paraphrase Neil Armstrong when he stepped on the surface of the moon in 1969, what is a small step for you and the kids in your class can lead to a giant step for mankind and for the future of education. It's time. It's time for us to do things differently and to stop offering education that meets the needs of only a small percentage of the learners in our classrooms.

When Neil Armstrong and NASA set forth to see what lay outside the sphere of our planet, they ended up learning dozens of things that changed our lives forever. From scratch-resistant glasses to water purification, our lives have been enriched by people who were brave enough to explore new frontiers. Just as universal design in architecture has made buildings more useable, more comfortable, and more efficient for everyone, CAST tells us that what we learn today while trying to teach the kids "on the margins" may change everything in education down the line (Meyer & Rose, 2005). And it's you, the teacher with a sense of adventure, the teacher who isn't afraid to try new things, the teacher with the passion to teach *everyone* in her class, who will make that first small step for children. What you do today changes everything in the future.

A PORTRAIT OF THE UDL CLASSROOM

Before I leave you, I'd like to take one more moment to revisit some of the wonderful students we met in Chapter 1 and paint a picture of what they are doing now. Let's imagine they are all in sixth grade, in a universally designed classroom taught by *you*. What would their school experience look like? Let's imagine . . .

First, let's look around your classroom. The desks are movable, so they can be arranged to face the front when students need to pay attention to the teacher and in small groups for cooperative work. There are resources such as word walls and checklists on the walls, but there isn't too much visual clutter; you know that some of your students get overwhelmed if there is too much visual stimulation.

Right now students are working on drafts of their writing projects about the American government. They are working on several Common Core standards, but the main one they are focused on for this project is W.6.2: Writing informative text to examine a topic and convey ideas. Over the last few weeks, you have systematically taught them to use a compare/ contrast graphic organizer, and they are using it today to write about the three branches of government (W.6.2.A). You have asked them to pay careful attention to the transitions in their piece (W.6.2.C), and because this is a stellar UDL classroom, the students are working on their projects in a variety of different ways.

Each student is allowed to pick three writing projects per semester to present in a completely different format—for instance, as a video, a cartoon, a speech, etc. Raymond, our friend from Chapter 1 who had difficulties with graphomotor skills, is working with his friend Sammy to write the script for a news broadcast about the branches of government. They are using Dragon Dictate, the speech-to-text app on Raymond's phone, to dictate the first draft of the script. After editing and revising, they will eventually use the camera on his phone to make a video of their script.

© monkeybusinessimages/Thinkstock

If we look over at the far corner of the room, we can see five or six students working with iPads at their desks. Included in this group is Dafne, our young friend with autism who struggled to remember what she wanted to write. Dafne is using a voice-recording app to record herself brainstorming ideas. She will then go back and transcribe those ideas into the graphic organizer that the class has been learning, and from there, she will record her first draft. For Dafne, using a voice recorder to write helps support her memory issues and motivates her to do her best work. Other students are using speech-to-text functions or text prediction as they compose on the iPads.

Do you remember Brian, who got so overwhelmed by the cognitive demands of writing that he forgot how to write the letter K? He is typing away on a laptop alongside a bunch of other students, including Roschan, who has difficulties with spatial organization. For Brian, Roschan, and many other of your students, the simple of act of using a computer to plan and write the content reduces the cognitive demands to the point where they can work effectively and produce their best writing. Usually about half of the class chooses to write on laptops, and you feel that this is good preparation for the demands of college and the working world.

In another part of the room, Carla and Toby are working together on a computer doing partner writing. As you might recall, Carla is the student whose short-term memory made it terribly difficult for her to copy words from the board, and Toby is the student whose long-term memory problems made word recall a serious issue for him. They take turns typing for each other, which reduces the cognitive demands and helps them each concentrate on the task of generating and organizing their thoughts. Before they began writing, you helped the class create a bank of academic vocabulary words that Carla and Toby have open on a Word document, and when they need one of those words, they can copy and paste it straight into their document. This helps both of them use grade-appropriate vocabulary in their writing instead of the low-level words that they were using previously. Two other pairs of students have chosen to do partner writing and are working quietly nearby. Both pairs have chosen to use pen and paper for this assignment, but they are still taking turns transcribing each other's words, and they have a copy of the word bank nearby.

Three students are creating comic strips. Among those is Sandra, our friend from Chapter 1 who struggles significantly with language. The three students are working together to decide how best to organize the big ideas for their projects, and they will be using bubbl. us to organize their ideas before they write. Finally, they will use the Bitstrips app to create their comic strips about the three branches of government.

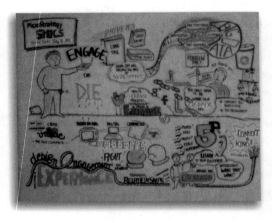

At the front of the class, a group of about ten students are working on the whiteboard to organize their ideas in a large, multicolored mind map. Stephen, who struggles with higher-order thinking, is participating in that group with enthusiasm. Stephen is an excellent artist, so the group has called upon him to illustrate the mind map. Once it's done, he will take the ideas from the mind map and work in a group to transcribe them into the graphic organizer that you have been teaching them. Then they will each individually translate that into a first draft. This very explicit process of brainstorming and organizing ideas with a group, then using a familiar graphic organizer to turn the ideas into a draft, helps Stephen and several other students make sense of the content and gives them support for the higher-level thinking this project demands.

As we can see, you have created a productive, lively classroom in which every student is exploring his or her own learning strengths. By giving them the opportunity to try out different techniques and tools for producing text, you have not only motivated and engaged them, but you've taught them which tools are most effective for their individual needs and what skills they need to develop. Your dynamic, energetic UDL classroom is teeming with students who are not only learning how to write, ***they are learning how to learn.***

And in the end, isn't that what we all want for our students?

FOR FURTHER READING

Downing, J. E. (2005). *Teaching literacy to students with significant disabilities: Strategies for the K–12 inclusive classroom.* Thousand Oaks, CA: Corwin.

Edyburn, D. L. (2005). Universal Design for Learning. *Special Education Technology Practice, 7*(5), 16–22.

Meyer, A., & Rose, D. H. (2005). The future is in the margins: The role of technology and disability in educational reform. In D. H. Rose, A. Meyer, & C. Hitchcock (Eds.), *The universally designed classroom: Accessible curriculum and digital technologies* (pp. 13–35). Cambridge, MA: Harvard Education Press. Retrieved from http://www.udlcenter.org/resource_library/articles/margins

References

Beck, I. L., McKeown, M. G., & Kucan, L. (2013). *Bringing words to life* (2nd ed.). New York, NY: Guilford.

Berninger, V. W., Nielson, K., Abbott, R., Wijsman, E., & Raskind, W. (2008). Writing problems in developmental dyslexia: Underrecognized and undertreated. *Journal of School Psychology, 46*(1), 1–21.

Burchers, S. (2007). *Vocabulary cartoons: SAT word power* (4th ed.). Punta Gorda, FL: New Monic Books.

Calkins, L., Ehrenworth, M., & Lehman, C. (2012). *Pathways to the Common Core: Accelerating achievement.* Portsmouth, NH: Heinemann.

Carroll, L. (1865/n.d.). *Alice's Adventures in Wonderland.* New York, NY: Carlton House.

CAST. (2012). Increase mastery-oriented feedback. Retrieved from http://www.udlcenter.org/implementation/examples/examples8_4

CAST. (2014). *Universal Design for Learning guidelines version 2.0.* Wakefield, MA: Author. Retrieved from http://www.udlcenter.org/aboutudl/udlguidelines

The Center for Universal Design. (1997). The principles of universal design (Version 2.0). Retrieved from http://www.ncsu.edu/ncsu/design/cud/about_ud/udprinciplestext.htm

Coleman, D. (2011, April). *Bringing the Common Core to life.* Paper presented at a meeting of the New York State Department of Education, Albany, NY.

Downing, J. E. (2005). *Teaching literacy to students with significant disabilities: Strategies for the K–12 inclusive classroom.* Thousand Oaks, CA: Corwin.

Edyburn, D. L. (2005). Universal Design for Learning. *Special Education Technology Practice, 7*(5), 16–22.

Ellis, E. S. (1992). *LINCS: A starter strategy for vocabulary learning.* Lawrence, KS: Edge Enterprises, Inc.

Gersten, R., & Baker, S. (2001). Teaching expressive writing to students with learning disabilities: A meta-analysis. *Elementary School Journal, 101*(3), 251–272.

Graham, S., & Harris, K. (2013). Common Core State Standards, writing, and students with LD: Recommendations. *Learning Disabilities Research & Practice, 28*(1), 28–37.

Greenwood, S. C., & Flanigan, K. (2007). Overlapping vocabulary and comprehension: Context clues complement semantic gradients. *Reading Teacher, 61,* 249–254.

Griffin, H. C., Williams, S. C., Davis, M. L., & Engleman, M. (2002). Using technology to enhance cues for children with low vision. *Teaching Exceptional Children, 35*(2), 36–42.

Harris, K. R., & Graham, S. (1996). *Making the writing process work: Strategies for composition and self-regulation.* Cambridge, MA: Brookline.

Harris, K. R., & Graham, S. (2013). "An adjective is a word hanging down from a noun": Learning to write and students with learning disabilities. *Annals of Dyslexia, 63,* 65–79.

Hougan, M. (2006). *Vocabulary strategies to improve comprehension.* Paper presented at California State University, Northridge, CA.

Hughes, L., & Wilkins, A. (2000). Typography in children's reading schemes may be suboptimal: Evidence from measures of reading rate. *Journal of Research in Reading, 23*(3), 314–324.

Kagan, S., & Kagan, M. (2009). *Kagan Cooperative Learning.* San Clemente, CA: Kagan Publishing.

Lavoie, R. (2007). *The motivation breakthrough: 6 secrets to turning on the tuned-out child.* New York, NY: Touchstone.

Lavoie, R., & Levine, M. (2005). *It's so much work to be your friend: Helping the child with learning disabilities find social success.* New York, NY: Touchstone.

Liu, C. H., & Matthews, R. (2005). Vygotsky's philosophy: Constructivism and its criticisms examined. *International Education Journal, 6,* 386–399.

Mastropieri, T., & Scruggs, M. (2014). *Thirty years of research collaboration: What have we learned and what remains to be learned?* Paper presented at the meeting of the Office of Special Education Programs Project Director's Conference, Washington, D.C.

McCormick, S., & Zutell, J. (2014). *Instructing students who have literacy problems* (6th ed.). Chicago, IL: Pearson.

Medina, J. (2014) (Updated and Expanded). *Brain rules: 12 principles for surviving and thriving at work, home, and school.* Seattle, WA: Pear Press.

Meyer, A., & Rose, D. H. (2005). The future is in the margins: The role of technology and disability in educational reform. In D. H. Rose, A. Meyer, & C. Hitchcock (Eds.), *The universally designed classroom: Accessible curriculum and digital technologies* (pp. 13–35). Cambridge, MA: Harvard Education Press. Retrieved from http://www.udlcenter.org/resource_library/articles/margins

Meyer, A., Rose, D. H., & Gordon, D. (2014). *Universal Design for Learning: Theory and practice.* Wakefield, MA: CAST.

National Center for Learning Disabilities. (n.d.). What is executive function? Retrieved from http://www.ncld.org/types-learning-disabilities/executive-function-disorders/what-is-executive-function

National Center for Learning Disabilities. (2011). *The state of learning disabilities.* New York, NY: Author. Retrieved from http://issuu.com/ncld/docs/state_of_ld?e=3297511/2624324#search

National Governors Association Center for Best Practices, Council of Chief State School Officers. (2010). *Common Core State Standards.* Washington, DC: Author.

Olinghouse, N., Graham, S., & Harris, K. R. (2010). Evidence-based writing practices at the primary and secondary/tertiary level. In M. Shinn, H. Walker,

& G. Stoner (Eds.), *Interventions for achievement and behavior in the three-tier model including RTI* (pp. 553–570). Washington, DC: National Association of School Psychologists.

Prensky, M. (2001). Digital natives, digital immigrants. *On the Horizon, 9*(5), 1–6.

Project Write (2009). TREE support materials. Retrieved from http://kc.vanderbilt .edu/projectwrite/tree-individual.html

Rasinski, T., Padak, N., Newton, R. M., & Newton, E. (2008). *Greek & Latin roots: Keys to building vocabulary.* Huntington Beach, CA: Shell Education.

Repertoire Productions (Producer). (2013). *The myth of average: Todd Rose at Tedx Sonoma County.* Retrieved from https://www.youtube.com/watch? v=4eBmyttcfU4

Rose, D. H., Hasselbring, T. S., Stahl, S., & Zabala, J. (2005). Assistive technology and universal design for learning: Two sides of the same coin. In D. Edyburn, K. Higgins, & R. Boone (Eds.), *Handbook of special education technology research and practice* (pp. 507–518). Whitefish Bay, WI: Knowledge by Design.

Santangelo, T., Harris, K. R., & Graham, S. (2008). Using self-regulated strategy development to support students who have "trubol giting thangs into werds." *Remedial and Special Education, 29,* 78–89.

Schunk, D. H. (1985). Participation in goal setting: Effects on self-efficacy and skills of learning disabled children. *Journal of Special Education, 19,* 307–317.

Stanovich, K. E. (1986). Matthew effects in reading: Some consequences of individual differences in the acquisition of literacy. *Reading Research Quarterly, 21,* 360–406.

Swanson, H. L., & Berninger, V. W. (1996). Individual differences in children's writing: A function of working memory or reading or both processes? *Reading and Writing: An Interdisciplinary Journal, 8,* 357–383.

TED Talks (Producer). (2013). *How to escape education's death valley: Sir Ken Robinson at TED Talks Education.* Retrieved from http://www.ted.com/talks/ ken_robinson_how_to_escape_education_s_death_valley#t-1278

Index